AT HOME
IN THE
WILDERNESS

*Color picture on cover reproduced by the kind permission of
Arnie Eklund and the Baha'i Great Council Fire Committee
of Washington*

By

SUN BEAR

Dedication

In this day and age of fast travel and hurried ways of living, there is still some rebellion against time-clock automation. Some of us after being laid off our jobs, or hearing the death knell to another Summit Conference, decide that civilization is not all it's cracked up to be, and that life in Smogville, U.S.A. or any of its sister cities gives no promise of a rosy future. Perhaps your folks lived on a farm or up in the bush country, or you have lived there in the past. Maybe one of you senior citizens has been retired or is out of a job at forty-five because you're considered too old for factory work.

Maybe you are an ex-Boy Scout that remembers learning about Indian lore and woodcraft, or you are a man that has been working on the job with an occasional weekend fishing or hunting trip over the years. As my people say, " 'The Indian at heart' is the one that would like to learn the ways of the wilderness."

For you this book is written.

SUN BEAR

ISBN 0-87961-004-2

Copyright © 1968, 1973, by Sun Bear
Nineteenth printing, 2003

Naturegraph Publishers has been publishing books on natural history, Native Americans, and outdoor subjects since 1946. Please write for our free catalog.

Books for a better world

Naturegraph Publishers, Inc.
PO Box 1047 • 3543 Indian Creek Rd
Happy Camp, CA 96039
(530) 493-5353
www.naturegraph.com

Table of Contents

Illustrators

Don G. Kelley .... Don GK

Janice Kirk .... J.E.K.

Lynn Maxwell .... LM

Emily Reid .... ER

David Spohn .... d.s.

List of Illustrations

Introduction

INDIAN LORE FOR LIVING WITH THE LAND:

To live with the land means understanding it and the things around you. You must think of yourself as one of the Great Spirit's creatures of the wilderness. The land has no enemies in it. You all share the same earth. You learn to live and blend with nature. You never kill anything that you don't eat. If you follow this way, you will always have food. The wilderness around you is your store house and refrigerator. The Indian refers to the animals as our Little Brothers, and we always would offer a prayer of thanks-giving when going on the hunt. "We have to take your life, Little Brother, in order to continue our own" was his prayer. Even when gathering herbs and plants for medicine or food, the Indian would never take the first plant he came to, but leave that one to insure survival of the species. He was a supreme conservationalist. His love of the outdoors and his thoughtfulness of and dependence upon the land made him think thus of it.

If you wish to live in the wilderness, follow the example left by the American Indian. Learn to love and understand it. Find beauty, not fear, in its storms and deserts. Seek to blend with nature, and not to conquer it. Find a sense of belonging and oneness with the land. You can learn from the things around you. See how the birds and animals use their natural coloring to conceal themselves when hunting or hiding out from enemies. Watch your Little Brothers again and they will lead you to water that is good to drink. They will tell what is good to eat in strange land too. You can watch them and see what fruits are edible. It is also this sense of belonging that kept the Indian from worrying when away from his home camp. He would say "Indian not lost, tepee lost." He never felt lost in his beautiful forest or plains. His ability to track animals was tremendous. Not only could he identify tracks in the snow and sand, but even by the broken leaves or bent grass, he could tell what creatures of the forest had passed there.

In raising his own food he developed $5/7$ of the vegetables that the world has today. His knowledge of farming was such that he disturbed the rich topsoil as little as possible, and in this way he preserved it from blowing away. Also he believed in feeding the ground with waste fish and other fertilizers. His patience and his love of the wilderness gave him a sense of balance. With this feeling he could live and travel for long periods alone. He learned to improvise so that he required very little equipment when traveling or hunting. The station wagon or camper hunter would be surprised at this skill. He also built up the country that was his. I have seen the old timers take choke cherry or plum seeds which they found growing in one area and plant same near a spring or creek where none grew, so there might be some there as well.

With no drug store handy, he learned the use of the herbs and plants that are used today by medical doctors and drug stores. The only difference is that today you buy them in bottles with labels.

The Indian regarded the earth as belonging to the Great Spirit, and himself as the caretaker only. "The land is mine only to use but it belongs to the Great Spirit and is for the use of generations to come." His willingness to share and give to his fellow man was a wonderful thing. Often he would give from behind a mask or unknown to the receivers so that they would think of it as a gift coming from the Great Spirit and not from the giver. He had true social security in the type of mutual assistance pact that functioned between him and his fellow men.

When a man got married everyone pitched in and helped him build a home, so that he had a house of his own and not a $20,000 mortgage for the rest of his life. If he went hunting or fishing and had more than he needed, he shared with others. His sense of not being rushed gave him mental health as well as physical health, and because of his faith and behavior the Great Spirit blessed him with many days, and he grew old, living a good life. May you do as well, my friends.

SUN BEAR

CHAPTER I

Vegetable and Fruit Raising

For a person going into the country or timber territory, whether he is going there for the summer or to live the year around, I think it's good to think of supplying a part of the food from vegetable and fruit raising. Of course what you will plant depends on your taste and food habits. How much depends on the size of your family and how much you will be depending on the garden for food. If you raise your own potatoes as well, it will take more ground. Your garden and fruit patch, for a family of four, will be from one-half to one and one-half acres in area.

A compost pile has two important functions. One, it is a place to dispose of "wet garbage" such as pea pods, watermelon rinds, cleared-up brush, egg shells, even fish or meat scraps. Two, the decayed material from the bottom of the compost pile provides many of the minerals taken out of the ground by growing vegetables.

A compost pile is started by digging a shallow area out. One foot deep and about 25 square feet is a good size. Use the earth removed from the area to build up the sides a little.

Your wet garbage is then thrown in at random. Rain water will help it decay. From time to time, turn your compost material with a pitchfork. This material will be worked into your garden when you get ready to plant in the spring.

Use varieties native to your area or that thrive there. Insure your crop in that way. Seed catalogs often describe the characteristics of each variety.

As soon as you move onto a place, plant your nut and fruit trees, as it takes from three to five years for them to produce a crop. It is best not to transplant during the winter months when the sap is down because any damaged roots would cause the tree to bleed to death. Be sure there is a cone of earth in the center of the hole which is prepared for a tree. This is to avoid any air pockets under the tree. If there is an air pocket, the tree just refuses to grow. It will not die but remain in the exact state as when it was first planted in the ground. Pour water in the hole first to be sure there is plenty of moisture. Set the tree on top of the cone and spread the roots evenly about it and

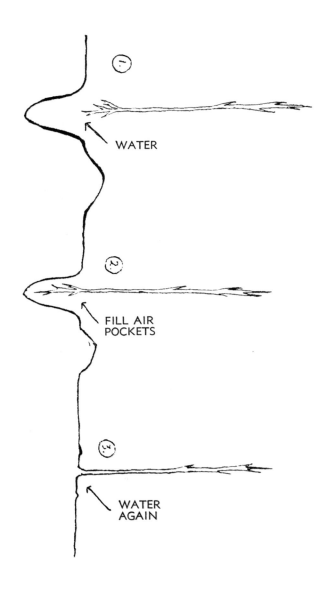

Planting Fruit Trees

down the sides. Fill dirt in a little at a time, making sure there are no clods or large chunks to create air pockets. Water it again thoroughly and do not water it again for one week except in hot weather.

Plant an assortment of plums, apples and grapes. Sometimes you will find a wild plum or berry patch from which to start your home orchard. These fruits, however, have a tendency to be all pit and no fruit. They will also taste of the pit. If you can graft a tree, then by all means start from a seedling root.

Berry shoots can be taken anytime after the fruit has been harvested and before the leaves fall. Transplanting wild berries is comparatively easy as they are very hardy and will not die because of broken roots. The main thing is to get the entire tap root. This is the long one in the center of the plant. Be very careful not to break it because this will cause the plant to bleed to death.

Slips should be cut back about four or five buds and always cut below an outside (away from the tree) bud. This bud will send the next branch outward rather than inward. The slip should be at least one foot long because there is quite a bit of die-back on berry and grape vines. For easy accessibility after your plants have started growing, start them on a trellis or arbor so both sides of the vine can be reached. This will produce more fruit.

Protecting young fruit trees from gnawing rabbits is important. Annie's mom used to cut the top and bottom away from a wax-coated milk carton, and use the rest around the tree to discourage the fuzzy little critters. A wire mesh cylinder is a variation of the same idea.

A strong solution of epsom salts is used by some people around their trees to get rid of rabbits. It does, but it isn't very nice.

One planting rule of one of our old-timers is that the vegetables that grow under the ground should be planted in the dark of the moon and ones growing above the ground should be planted in the light of the moon. The reason for this is that if the tuburous plants are planted in the light of the moon, they will be all tops and no bottoms. The reverse is true of the plants that grow above the earth. Watch the moon. If it is just a "crust of the cookie", so to speak, then it is the dark moon and you must get your tuburous vegetables in the ground before it has once again become big and full. When the moon is big and full, then it's time to plant your leafy vegetables before the moon goes dark again.

Laying Out Garden—Use Sunshine and Rain to the Best Advantage

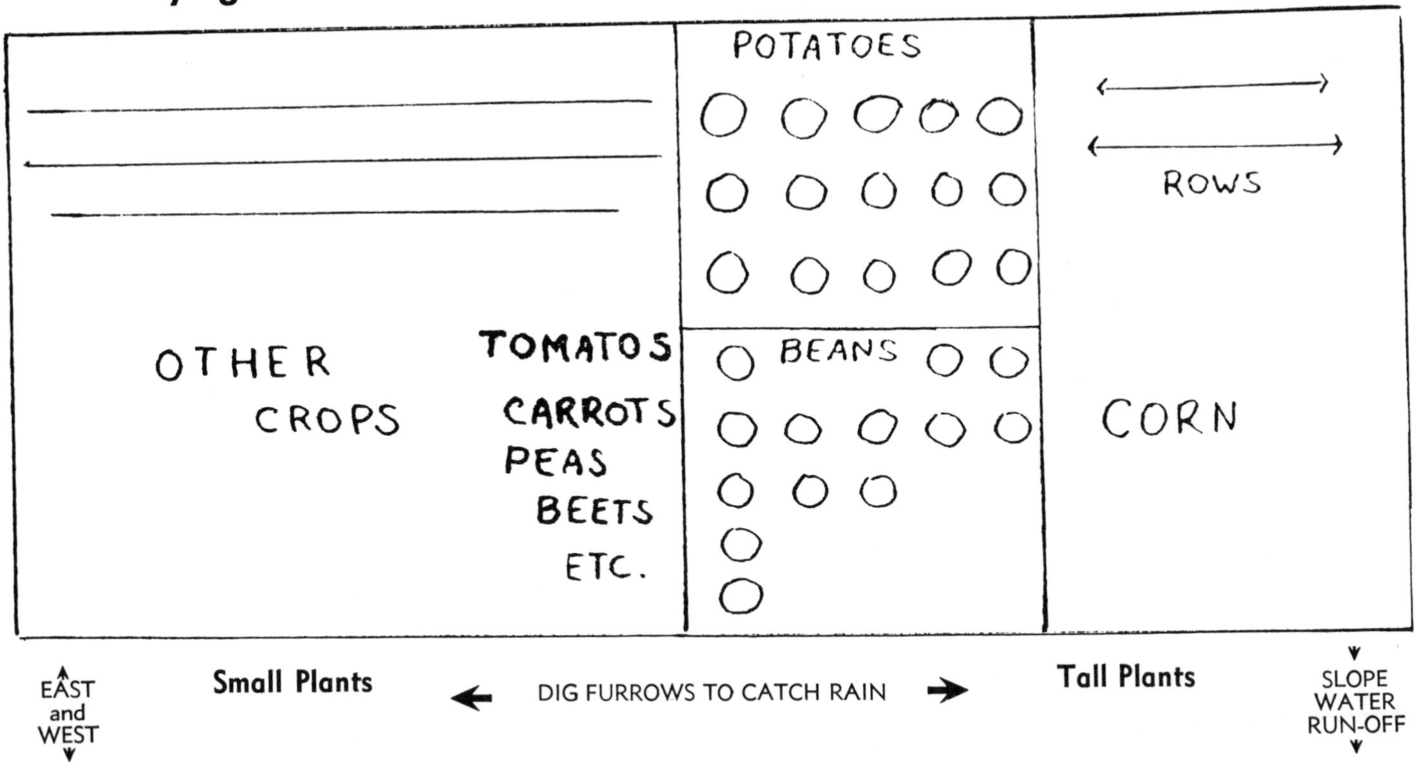

Rows

POTATOES

CORN

BEANS

OTHER CROPS

TOMATOS
CARROTS
PEAS
BEETS
ETC.

EAST and WEST

Small Plants

DIG FURROWS TO CATCH RAIN

Tall Plants

SLOPE WATER RUN-OFF

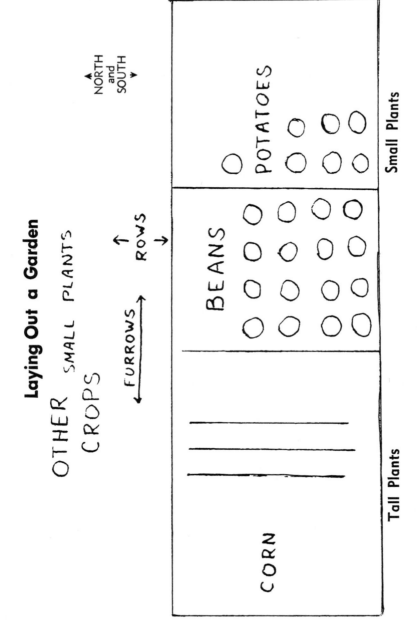

Laying Out a Garden

Small Plants

Tall Plants

Rutabagas may be planted as a substitute for potatoes, for when potatoes become diseased, you still have rutabagas for that year. They provide as much nutrition. For the summer you can enjoy fresh vegetables such as radishes and lettuce, cabbage, tomatoes, cucumbers, carrots, and beets. All of these except lettuce and radishes can be pickled. I raise mainly corn, beans (for drying and green beans), peas, squash, pumpkins, rutabagas, potatoes, and carrots because they are best to store and keep and are easily canned along with strawberries, raspberries or blackberries.

PLANT

BETWEEN

FURROWS

There are some varieties of vegetables that are more hardy, which means they can stand colder weather or even light frost. Some can stand more dry weather. When you buy seeds, I suggest you consult a seedman. If you look in farm magazines you will see seed companies offering their catalogs which are usually sent free. To me there is no joy like looking over a beautifully illustrated seed catalog. (You city dwellers, what you will miss until you discover this treat!)

CORN

When planting corn, plant it in rows 3 feet apart. Put 4 kernels to the hill and the hills 3 feet apart in the row. Once the corn has sprouted and is about 4 inches tall, you must go down the rows and thin out the extras. Only two stalks to a hill is the maximum for good production. When they have grown to about waist high, once again you must go down the rows and cut away the suckers or stalks that grow from the main stalk that otherwise will take away from the size of the ears of the corn. Small and stinted ears will be the yield if the suckers are allowed to remain. The small ears of corn have more trouble with silk worms than larger hardier ones. I sometimes plant pumpkin or squash between the stalks of corn, 2 seeds to every hill for the amount I want. The land thus serves a double purpose. If you have no use for the corn stalk after it has been harvested, leave it stand in the field and plant your climbing beans there the next year.

This is the way my grandmother and her folks before her always planted it. They were the first agriculturalists on this continent and started the cultivation of corn and squash. Better teachers are not to be found.

We usually hoe up dirt around the corn and squash plants in little hills. This gives them support and protects the roots from the hot wind and sun. The seeds should be planted about 3 1/2 inches deep. I soak mine in water overnight to speed up germination. I also do this with corn, beans, peas, squash, pumpkins, cucumbers, watermelons, muskmelons, and Sunflowers.

BEANS

Do not plant beans until the cold, wet weather is over, then set them in rows 20 inches apart. Put them in 2 inches deep with four beans to a hill, a foot apart in the row. Do not cultivate or work around plants when the ground is wet or the plants will rust when they get splattered with wet soil.

PEAS

Sow early in the spring in rows 20 inches apart covering one and one half to two inches deep. One pound of peas will plant two 50-foot rows. Remember to plant them in the light of the moon.

SQUASH AND PUMPKINS

Plant them in hills about 4 or 6 feet apart. Cover the seeds about one and one half inches. Put 4 or 6 seeds to the hill. Plant in the spring after frost danger is over.

MELONS AND CUCUMBERS

Plant them the same way you do squash and pumpkins.

TOMATOES

You may plant the seeds outside after the danger of frost has passed for a later crop, or you can start the seeds in a flat box in the house and transplant them outside after the plants are six to ten inches high if you want an earlier crop. It is easy to make your own hot house for germinating seeds. Build a frame of wood the size of a house door, and two or three feet deep. Fill the frame with equal parts of cow manure and dirt and mix them thoroughly. Put the seeds thinly in this mixture and stir lightly with a table fork. Place an old glass door, such as a french door over this or cover it with thin plastic. Water the seeds every day, and when you water them be sure to use a very fine, light spray so you do not disturb the seed.

This can be done outside before the last frost and your plants will be ready for planting just in time. Plant them in rows four feet apart each way. It sometimes becomes necessary to brace up the plants as they become loaded with fruit.

CARROTS, ONIONS, TURNIPS, BEETS AND RUTABAGAS

These are all planted in rows 20 inches apart with the seeds about one half inch deep. They can be planted early because they are more frost resistant. They should be thinned out when they start growing because they are planted close together. Turnips and rutabagas may be planted in May or June for a fall crop. Broadcast them thinly in lightly prepared soil. If you want, you can broadcast them on upturned soil as long as it is weed free. The crop will be ready about the last of September, just in time to avoid the first frost in cold country.

The radish and onion, if allowed, will go to seed. You may harvest this seed and use it for the following season.

POTATOES

In planting potatoes, cut the large seed potatoes in half leaving an eye for each half. The eye is the place where the sprout forms which makes the potato plant. You may plant the small ones whole. If you wish, you may just cut out the eye with a chunk of the potato about the size of a tablespoon and save the rest to eat during the spring before your crop comes in. This is a good way to do it in depression, or recession, as they call it now.

Plant potatoes in rows two feet apart. The plants should be in hills 16 inches apart in the row. An easy measurement is to plow the ground with a double plow. Place off the planting space by taking a normal step, then drop the potato eye by your heel. The eye should be covered by approximately six inches of dirt.

If potato bugs get started in them it will be before the blossom comes on. They may be picked off by hand and killed by putting them in kerosene, or the plant may be sprayed with Parish Green poison or with more readily available arsenic of lead powder which is mixed with water and sprayed on, or dusted on as it is. Above all, do not allow the bugs to remain on the potato plants or they will completely destroy it. Check for eggs on the underside of the leaf. They will be orange in color and there will be as many as 50 or 75 eggs in a bunch. Occasionally there will be as few as three or four in a spot. These eggs are as small as the head of a straight pin and are in small bunches that are easy to overlook. Be sure to reach these spots when you dust or spray.

Picking potato bugs is a good job for the children.

HARVEST

Dry beans and peas should be harvested in the fall before the rain starts. The bush and all is harvested. To thrash them out, a large galvanized tub can be used. Fill the tub with the whole bushes about one-third full. Stand in it and stamp the beans free.

Another way is to use a burlap sack. Fill it half full and tie the end. Then stamp on it or pound it with a club. An easier way yet is to spread the stalks in a shed with a wooden floor and use bamboo rakes as thrashers.

Then gather the large stems from the threshed beans, regardless of the method you use. You are ready for the winnowing now.

Annie recalls thrashing beans on the barn floor with a bamboo rake. When the bushes were removed to the compost pile, the beans were left on the floor, ready to be gathered up and used.

A flat basket or grading screen such as is used in grading sand in cement may be used. Pour the beans and chaff which is loose in the container used for threshing. Shift them from one basket or grading screen to the other, holding them about two to two and a half feet apart. This should be done on a windy day because the wind is a great help in removing the chaff. Peas can be threshed in this way also.

A good thing to know in this uncertain atomic age when one day you may be working, and the next day, a change-over may put you out of work, is how to survive this way. It gives one a feeling of confidence to be able to know how to work with his hands. He is dependent upon his own ability.

NOTE: Many people feel that botanically derived sprays and powders are intrinsically safer than the Paris Green poison or arsenic lead powder mentioned on the preceeding page. Pyrethrin and rotenone are two plant-derived substances worthwhile for the reader to inquire about. Powdered tobacco is recommended by the author.

SHELVES

BIN

DRAIN

MEAT HANGER

T.

DOOR

BIN

HILLSIDE ROOT CELLAR FOR FOOD STORAGE

CHAPTER II

The Root Cellar

A root cellar is very important when you raise your own vegetables and fruits. It functions in several ways. It is used to store your tuberous vegetables, fresh and canned food, and in some cases, serves as a storm cellar. It is comparatively simple to construct, although it takes a lot of hard work with a shovel.

First you dig a pit about the size of an average size room in a house, about 9 x 12 feet and at least 6 or 7 feet deep, and deeper on one end than the other. This is normally lined with sand and rock, the sides of which support themselves. However, if you have cement to use as mortar, river rock (which is smoother than ordinary rock) is very nice to use. Drains must be forced into the bottom of the wall on the deeper end, about two feet deep. This is so seepage water will not stand in the finished cellar.

Build a flight of stairs or ladder on the shallow end reaching to the ground, and line this also with sand rock or river rock. Don't cement the entire inside surface. Rock gives the desired coolness. Cement does not get as cold as rocks. After the walls, floor, and stairway have been lined with rock, place fallen timbers of hard wood, (preferably green wood, as dry wood will soon rot) over the top, level with ground, forming a roof. They must be placed side by side because rock will be shoveled on the top, about two or three feet thick. The entire roof is then to be covered with dirt about one foot thick.

When you build a frame for a door covering for the stairway, be sure it will be tight and let in as little light as possible. Sometimes it is advisable to make two doors, one at the bottom of the stairs and the other at the top opening. When you have shelves for canned goods, and bins lined with good wheat straw, your cellar is finished.

The purpose of the cellar is to preserve your vegetables. A cold, dark place is best for storage in every instance. Milk and eggs can be set there as well. Your potatoes, rutabagas, carrots, cabbage, beets, onions, pumpkins, squash, and melons will be stored here. Be sure to pack everything but the potatoes in straw with the root side of the vegetable turned up because it will sprout if the root side is down. Be careful to pack the vegetables well so they do not touch each other, because they will rot where they touch if they are left long enough.

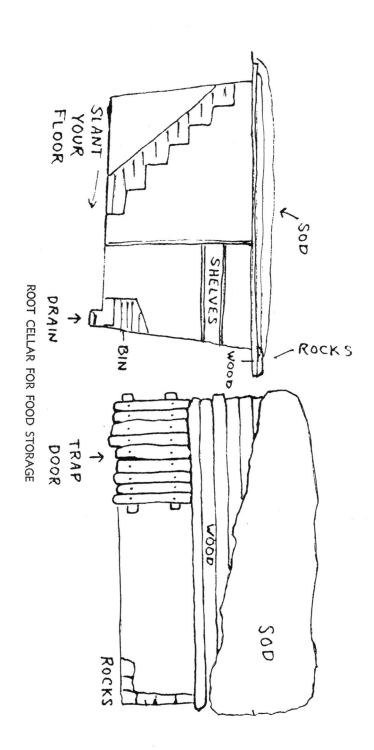

ROOT CELLAR FOR FOOD STORAGE

CHAPTER III

Preservation of Food

In this day and age, we have several choices open to us for food preservation. If you have a garden of your own, have fruit trees, or raise your own meat, you will be able to feed your family on much less than city people are able to do. You must be willing to invest your time, and learn the best methods for certain foods to preserve their flavor and quality and keep them safe for consumption.

It is possible to preserve foods by canning, freezing, drying, or smoking and pickling.

Today, people are discovering that freezing of foods, both raw and cooked, is easier than canning and preserves color, texture and flavor better. It makes it possible to take advantage of quantity buying when foods are in season, or when special sales are available. It is possible to freeze leftovers for use at another time or to prepare in advance for holiday or company meals. Wise use can make it possible for any family to eat better on less money and conserve the time of the person for other activities.

HOME CANNING

There are different methods of canning food; cold packing, pressure canning, and open kettle canning. Be sure to follow the correct directions. Cook books, libraries, farm extension services all have material to help the inexperienced.

Please do not always follow the practices that may have been used in your area in the past or by homemakers years ago. We now know through scientific research the dangers that can occur and that the bacteria causing botulism may now be present in your soil when this was not so in the past. It can be carried from place to place and infect the soil, and if your canned food contains this bacteria, it will grow in the presence of moisture and heat in the container to become very poisonous and deadly. Many times in the past people have eaten vegetables or meat improperly processed and not become ill because the soil was not infected BUT YOU CAN NOT BE SURE.

It is possible to destroy the toxin in a home canned vegetable or meat that has not been pressure cooked by boiling at 212° F. for five minutes. At higher altitudes, boiling temperature is lower, so do not use the fact that it is boiling as an indication that it is 212 degrees.

HOWEVER, this excess boiling destroys most of the vitamins and food value of the vegetables and this additional cooking destroys its attractiveness so this method is not recommended.

Processing in a pressure canner is the only method approved for canning vegetables and meat. Follow the manufacturer's directions carefully.

Fruits and tomatoes contain enough acid so they can be processed safely in a boiling water bath canner by the cold pack method or by the open kettle method. Canning juices without sugar is possible. They may be used to make up into fresh jelly during the winter, or may be used for fruit drinks, and sauces.

Select clean, sound, fully ripe fruit that is uniform in size. Wash thoroughly and prepare according to directions. Prepare only enough for one canner load or "batch" at one time.

Before starting the canning process, inspect your jars carefully and discard any with even a tiny nick. Large mouthed jars are easy to fill. The vacuum-seal metal covers are easiest to use, with new covers for each canning. Wash the jars thoroughly and rinse. Keep the jars, tops in warm water until ready to fill.

Pack to within $\frac{1}{2}$ inch of the top. Pack vegetables loosely, especially corn, shell beans and peas. Pack fruit as tightly as possible without crushing. Press tomatoes down to get juice. Add $\frac{1}{2}$ teaspoon salt for each pint vegetables. For fruit, use either thin, medium or heavy syrup which has been precooked. This is added to the jar boiling hot. It is possible to can fruit without sugar (except strawberries) but it will not be as firm or the flavor as good.

For open kettle canning fruits, they should be cooked in a syrup made of 1 cup of sugar, 1 cup of water, and 1 tablespoon of corn syrup. Then place the cooked fruit directly into the jars. Fill the jars while the fruit is boiling and seal them tightly. Remember to always wipe off the top of the jar before trying to seal it because it will not seal properly if you do not.

Do not tighten any loose rings you might discover. This will break the seal. Just leave them until you have need for the ring as it can be removed without breaking the seal. Many times you may be short of rings. Never remove a tightly set ring, unless you are prepared to use the vegetable.

Here are some recipes that you might like to try instead of canning.

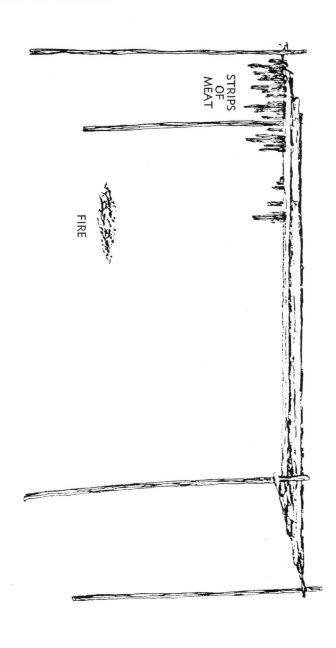

STRIPS
OF
MEAT

FIRE

JERKING MEAT

JERKEY OR CHARQUE: Build stick platforms about 4 or 5 feet high. Cut the raw meat into long, thin slices and hook them upon the platform so that the slices do not touch. In dry countries the hot sun will dry the meat in 4 or 5 days but in the more cloudy or rainy country sometimes it becomes necessary to build a fire under the racks to help with the drying. Jerkey can be dried with 4 or 5 days of steady smoking. Remember to cover your jerkey at night with sufficient material to keep the night wetness off the meat or it will spoil. Another method of making jerkey is to salt and pepper it heavily. This keeps the insects off the drying meat. This type of jerkey should be parboiled before you try to use it. Too much salt may be undesirable.

When salting pork or other meats such as fish, deer, or beef, use rock salt, which is sometimes called ice cream salt by the old timers. Be very careful that the pieces of meat do not touch each other, or it will spoil rather than cure in the salt. Wooden kegs are more desirable but earthenware can be used. Never use metal containers.

Pork can be fried and stored in its own grease. Sausage is very nice on cold mornings with potatoes and gravy. Just dig it out of the grease already prepared and heat it. It will not spoil as long as it is placed in your root cellar and covered with a wooden slab or cover.

Dried fish is made much in the same way jerkey is made. Clean the fish thoroughly before hanging it out to dry. Salted fish can be kept for years. Non-salted fish can be cooked in many appetizing ways.

Pemmican is made from jerkey meat. Take 5 pounds of jerked meat and grind it into a meal-like substance, add $\frac{1}{2}$ pound of brown sugar and $\frac{3}{4}$ pound raisins or dried currants. The Chippewas used blueberries or June berries for this. Mix the ingredients all together and then add 4 lbs melted suet. Pemmican can be stored in hide or canvas bags. The canvas bags can be made waterproof with parafin and a hot iron. Pemmican will keep for many months in this form and can be eaten raw or fried.

Meat may also be preserved by corning it. Prepare a brine by adding fine salt to boiling water until it will hold up a potato. A little saltpeter may add to the color of the meat, but will do nothing to the flavor or quality. Pack the meat in a tub and cover it with the cool brine solution.

CORN

Preserving corn without canning it in fruit jars is an art practiced only among the Indians. Usually, green corn is cut from the ear and roasted in a slow oven until it is hard, but some Indians first roast it on the ear and then cut it off and dry it. It must be spread thinly on a sheet or container. It can also be dried on rocks or on the roof, if you protect it from the birds, as they will eat more than you can prepare. When you wish to use your Indian dried corn, simply put it to soak over night, and the next morning, put in a piece of your salt pork and boil it as you would a kettle of beans. It will return to its original shape but will have an entirely different flavor.

Many fruits and vegetables may be dried. We have successfully dried apples, peaches, apricots, pears, figs, tomatoes, carrots, zucchini squash, cabbage, cherries and prunes.

To prepare apples wash the fruit, then cut out all worm holes. Slice in slices about one-quarter inch thick. We leave on the peelings and core, and slice crossways, although you could also cut the apple into eights. Place the slices on drying racks or cardboard boxes cut low. Make sure the fruit does not touch.

Peaches and apricots are prepared by washing, cutting off the bad spots, cutting in half and removing pits, and then placing the uncut surface on drying boards. Again, be careful that there is space between each piece of fruit.

Tomatoes: Cut the smaller ones in quarters, and larger ones into eights or even sixteenths. Take out all bad spots, then put on your drying rack.

Cherries: Cut in half, pit, put on drying racks.

Pears: Slice in halves or quarters, cut out the bad spots and dry.

Figs: When they fall from the trees pick them up and just dry.

Prunes: Can be prepared with or without the pit. One of our friends pokes his prunes with a fork after they have dried for a day as they swell up by that time. Any holes let prunes dry faster.

Zucchini, carrots, onions, cabbage, etc: Just slice in thin slices and place on drying racks. They go good with dried tomatoes in your winter stew.

When we have dried our fruits and vegetables, we put them in the freezer for about two days in order to kill bacteria or insects in them. Then we put them in plastic bags, keeping the amount in each bag small so if one portion molds it doesn't wipe out our whole supply. Then put into a tin or jar. You can skip the plastic bags if you wish. Keep fruits or vegetables dry and they will keep indefinitely.

CHAPTER IV

Good Outdoor Recipes

Camp measurements may be a little unorthodox, but they are very good rules to follow. A handful is the quantity obtained by using the hand as a scoop, filling it as full as possible. In using dry materials like baking powder, use the number of fingers called for, holding them tightly together. Lift the ingredient out with finger and thumb without turning it, some of the ingredients falls back into the container and the full measurement is not obtained. For a finger of fat, use one finger as a scoop.

NAVAJO WAR BREAD: You need no pans for this bread. Take one heaping teaspoon of baking powder and ½ a teaspoon of salt and mix in the dry flour in the middle of the sack. Then add water, a little at a time to avoid making lumps. Mix it until soft dough can be worked between floured hands.

At least a half hour before you are ready to bake, build a hardwood fire on a flat rock. When a good bed of coals has developed and the rock is well heated, brush away the coals and place the loaf, well covered with flour, upon the hot rock. Then cover the bread with hot ashes and over that put red hot coals. Test the bread with a straw or sliver from time to time. When the dough no longer adheres to the straw, the bread is done.

HARDTACK

Use 1 teaspoon of salt, 1 teaspoon of sugar, and about five cups of flour. Mix the dry ingredients and then add just enough water to make a stiff dough. Roll out the dough to about ¼ inch thick and cut it into sections. Bake them in a greased pan until the hardtack is bone dry.

SOURDOUGH BREAD

This type of bread was used in the gold rush days and a few miners were nicknamed Sourdough because of it. To make the sourdough ferment for the bread, mix 4 cups of flour with 3 teaspoons of sugar, 2 teaspoons of salt and about 3 or 4 cups of water. Use enough water to make a thick batter. Place this in a large container next to the fire and cover it. In two days it will have the odor of sourdough and will be ready to mix with your bread dough. Use about ¾ of the ferment for baking and save the remaining sourdough for a starter for another batch. Just add more flour and water and replace it behind the fire or stove. We always wrapped it in a flour sack to keep it from drying out.

To make sourdough bread, mix 1 tablespoon of melted lard, 1 cup of flour and 1 teaspoon of baking powder with the sourdough. Keep adding flour until it can absorb no more. Knead it until it is smooth and place the loaves in greased pans. Keep them warm until they have doubled in size. They can be baked in a reflector oven or in your oven at home. The baking eliminates the bad odor of the sourdough.

FLAPJACKS OR PANCAKES

You need 1 cupful of flour, ½ teaspoon of salt, and 1 heaping teaspoon of baking powder. Slowly add some water or milk. Add an egg at this point if you want. You can also add 2 teaspoons of melted fat. Spoon the batter into a hot pan and wait until bubbles appear on the top and it appears slightly dry around the edges. Turn it over and cook the other side. A dry pan is used when the fat is added to the batter. These with wild strawberries or blueberries is a real treat.

CORN PONE OR HUSH PUPPIES

Mix ½ a teaspoon of salt with 1 cup of cornmeal, ½ cup of cracklings and ¼ cup of corn. Add hot water until the swollen corn meal can be worked into a ball. Bake the stuff about 25 minutes. This is called hush puppies because on hunting trips hunters used to feed them to the dogs to keep them quiet because the dogs were not fed before a hunt.

CORN

Corn can be roasted over an open fire or boiled. Leave the husks on for roasting and boiling as it will enhance the flavor of the corn. The silks are easy to remove before eating.

CORN MEAL MUSH

Boil about 1 cup of corn meal, 1 teaspoon of salt and 3 cups of water. This can be used as a gruel or more often it is fried after the mush sets up. Pour it into a flat pan and smooth it out. Let it stand until it is stiff and cold. Cut it into cubes and fry it in smoking hot fat.

COFFEE can be made in several different ways.

Corn kernels roasted on coals may be pounded into a powder and boiled for coffee.

Sunflower coffee is made from roasted sunflower seeds. After they are roasted, the seeds and shells are separated, and boiling water is poured over the shells.

Wild coffee-bean trees can be found in the midwestern states. The beans, when roasted and ground, make a very delightful coffee. Some people like to add a little chicory.

Catalpa trees have long, slender pods after the massive blossoms have passed in the spring. These pods do not have beans inside them but the pods themselves are roasted and prepared much the same as tea, this is a good coffee substitute.

Barley coffee is made by washing the barley and placing it in a pan to roast. Molasses can be sprinkled on to improve the flavor. After roasting, crush and pound the mixture with a fork. When it was boiling, we used to put in a spoon of butter, because it keeps it from boiling over.

CHEWING GUM

Chewing Gum is a favorite with most Americans. There are a few places where this commodity may be found when you are camping and you have the urge to chew.

Spruce trees: Cut the bark and allow the sap to drain. It will harden enough that it will not stick to your teeth. If it is too hard, it will crumble.

Skeleton weed: It is a stiff plant related to wild lettuce, and it has pink flowers. Cut up the plant to allow the gum to come out. When it is hardened, it may be collected and chewed.

Rabbit Brush Gum: It has bluish green leaves and yellow flowers, and grows on the desert. Indians often used the yellow flowers as dye. The inner bark makes good chewing gum. This plant contains a small amount of rubber which assists in making the bark chewable.

Pine gum: The pitch from pine trees that are dead, mixed with bees wax makes very good chewing gum.

Rosin weed: This has yellow flowers 3 to 4 inches across resembling the wild sunflower. Alternate stem leaves usually point north and south and some call it a compass weed. Upper parts of the stem form large quantities of resinous material which is used as chewing gum.

MUSHROOMS

You may want to gather mushrooms, but there is danger in mushrooms even if there are pictures of them, so don't try it unless you are sure you know what you're doing.

CRAYFISH

Crayfish or crawdads can be eaten. Wash them in clean water and drop them into boiling water. They will turn a bright red much like a lobster. The tails taste a good deal like lobster.

MUSSELS

Mussels are plentiful and edible. To clean them, place them in a pot of cold water and they will open by themselves in a short time. If you don't want to get wet, stand away from them, as they will spit. After they are clean, drop them into boiling water to make them turn loose of the shell. The corn meal makes the mussel much more appetizing.

If you live on the Pacific Coast watch for posted shellfish quarantine signs—usually between May and November.

BEANS

In cooking beans, my friend Craig says that if you cook them at lower altitudes and then take them to the high country, you will have no trouble cooking them again when you get there. Boiling them first at a high altitude will not be successful. Before you get to a high altitude, boil them until they are soft, spread them out on a sheet or canvas to dry, and then pack them up for future cooking.

In packing into the woods, the dry soup mixes that you can buy for 10 cents an envelope are good and you can throw in whatever meat you kill to make stews.

CHIPPEWA SUCCOTASH

Use rice, wild or regular, or Indian dried corn. Chop your meat up fine, add cabbage, tomatoes, and season with onions. Use portions according to the number of people to feed. This recipe can be cooked on a stove or over a campfire as stew. It can also be baked in an oven as a hot dish.

CHAPTER V

Useful Edible Wild Plants and Herbs

Many people are inclined to raise their eye-brows and pooh-pooh vegetables, fruits or greens that they don't buy out of the super market. They forget that all of our domestic or cultivated plants came from wild ancestors. Even today in this country and in many others, one sees the cultivated crops growing in a field and the wild ones growing in the meadow or forest nearby. Many people would starve to death in the midst of a wilderness of plenty, for the lack of super market labels and identifying price tags, while my tribesmen find healthful food in the woodland berry patches, in roots and bulbs along the lakeshore, in sea weeds by oceanside, among the mountain pines, and even in the barren desert stretches.

TUMBLEWEED

Tumbleweed (also known as Russian Thistle) is a plant well-known throughout the western and mid-western states. In the fall of the year it's a familiar sight to see it broken loose from its roots and rolling across the field and plains, from which the name tumbleweed is given it. But if it's picked when 4 or 5 inches high when it has no thorns, it makes healthy greens. Pick it, cut off the roots and wash it in two or three waters to clean out dirt and sand. Put it in a pot with enough water to cover it. I sometimes put slices of bacon or pork in for flavor, and when serving it, I put a bottle of vinegar on the table for those who like it for seasoning.

DANDELION

This is perhaps our most common and most prolific food plant. Its leaves, boiled in two waters to remove the bitterness, may be served like spinach or beet tops, or its very young leaves may be made into a green salad. The French-Canadians dig up the roots and cut them into bitter salad. Dandelion greens have 25 times the Vitamin-A content of tomato juice, and 50 times that of asparagus.

CHICORY

Another common plant whose young leaves may be eaten raw or boiled as a potherb.

CHICORY

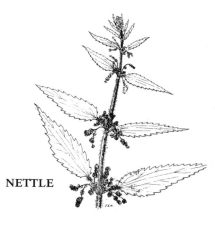

NETTLE

MUSTARD

MILKWEED

The young shoots of milkweed also may be boiled, although older stems are too acid and milky for use. Young pods are excellent when cooked.

MUSTARD

The young leaves of mustard, when cooked, add a special flavor to a mess of greens. Mustard aids digestion. Roots of this plant may be ground or pounded into a pulp for meat garnish. Some people boil it in two waters because they think it is bitter otherwise.

GREAT BURDOCK

When peeled, the tender shoots of burdock can be eaten raw, or may be made into a salad with oil and vinegar. If stripped of their outer peels, the stalks may be boiled or fried in butter or oil. The peeled roots may be sliced and boiled with salt and pepper. They also may be mashed and made into cakes and fried in butter. This plant is a great favorite among many of us. You find burdock around old abandoned buildings and manure piles.

CLOVER

The young plants, before the flowering stage, are eaten raw by Indians. Any digestive difficulties are overcome by dipping the leaves first in salt water.

CURLY DOCK

The young tender leaves of curley dock may be cooked. The seeds are ground and made into cakes or gruel. Also, the seeds can be used in place of tobacco.

FERNS

The fiddleheads, or young curled shoots of bracken cinnamon color make an excellent substitute for asparagus when boiled. Butter or hollandaise sauce may be poured over them. The fern should be boiled in salty water until tender.

LAMBS QUARTERS

This makes a fine summer potherb. It should be boiled in two waters which does away with any bad taste it may have. It is usually found in acid ground or damp areas.

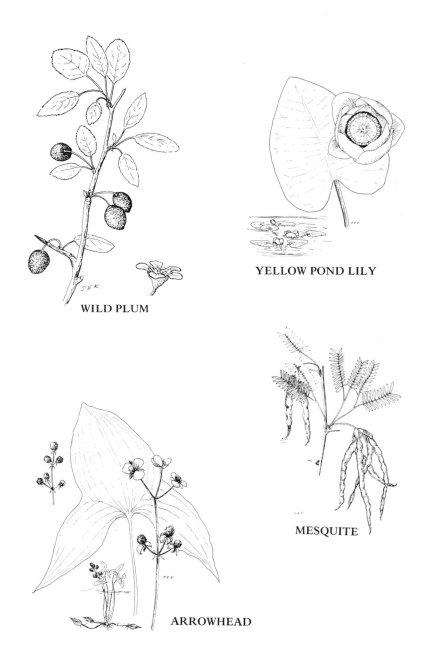

WILD PLUM

YELLOW POND LILY

MESQUITE

ARROWHEAD

MARSH MARIGOLDS

A favorite in the early days of the colonies. The young leaves of marsh marigolds were boiled into greens and the flower buds were pickled.

NETTLE

When gathering nettles, wear some protection on the hands, since they create a rash. The young plant, however will add a delicious flavor to other greens or soups when boiled. Older plants are called stinging nettles because of their numerous nettles or thorns.

BUTTERFLY WEED OR PLUERISY ROOT

The shoots may be cooked like asparagus. The root is edible when roasted.

YOUNG GRAPEVINE SHOOTS

These were eaten raw by the Seneca Indians of western New York, and the grapes were boiled into jelly.

EVENING PRIMROSE

Shoots may be eaten raw. The roots have a pleasant flavor and may be stewed like celery. This flavor blooms after sundown.

SKUNK CABBAGE

The young shoots of eastern skunk cabbage are boiled and the roots roasted.

VIOLETS

These were cultivated in the kitchen gardens for salads in Europe. Also boiled with a seasoning of savory and fennel in soups and stews. Early Blue Violet is still used by our southern Negroes to thicken soups and is called Wild Okra.

PALMETTO CABBAGE

This little palm does not grow very high and is found in North Carolina and Florida. The central leaves form a kind of cabbage and makes a very good vegetable. Be careful not to cut too much of the terminal bud, as it will kill the tree. The Seminole Indians make use of this plant.

WILD ONIONS

This is used by my Washoe friends in Nevada, and is a delicacy that surpasses all. Meats improve in flavor with a tiny bit of wild onion. This plant is easy to recognize. It grows not more than three or four inches tall and has a tiny, white, bellshaped flower on it. If you can't see, just smell.

WILD GARLIC

Wild Garlic has the appearance of small leeks and is very potent.

COW CABBAGE

This is a small sour plant that grows mostly in open places. It is a low growing plant that lays flat on the ground and you can distinguish it from all other low growing broad leafed plants by picking it. If it bleeds red, then it is the true cow cabbage and can be mixed in with other greens described herein. It is not advisable to eat this plant alone as its taste would be disagreeable, but mixed with others, it gives a flavor all of its own.

COW PEAS

These are called cow peas because the cows love them. They are usually ripe about the time green beans would be ready for picking. They can be eaten green or later when they are dry. Recently, these peas are being called blackeyed peas. They grow much the same as green peas only the bush is a little higher and does not send out tentacles to fasten onto other plants. The pods look like ordinary garden variety peas and hang from the underside of the bush.

FOX GRAPES

These are very sour and bitter when raw but make a very fine jam or jelly without any Sure-Jell or pectin, as they have their own gelatin. They look like any green Tokay grape you see growing in the fields of California, but they grow in the midwestern and southern states, mostly.

SAND HILL PLUMS

These are sweet and juicy when raw, and grow, as the name implies, in sand. They are yellow meated and pink color on the outside. If you try to cook them, be sure to have lots of sugar on hand, because they turn sour.

PERSIMMONS

Persimmons grow wild in some states and are gathered after the first frost and before the opossom and coon get to them. If you don't sit and wait for the frost to hit, the animals will have them and be gone, because they are a REAL treat. Green ones are worse than a mouth full of alum.

BLACK HAWS AND RED HAWS

These look a good deal like wild grapes hanging. They have a dried cherry taste. They are very hard to get, and you have to be an accomplished climber to get to them. They usually grow among the Black Jack Oak trees in the mid-western states.

PAW PAWS

Paw Paws are a wild banana with seeds like the loquat fruit of California. They have the taste of a fresh persimmon, but when made into a drink, they taste like the passion fruit from Hawaii. It is an exotic fruit that everyone should try, at least once in his life.

WILD TOMATOES

Wild tomatoes are about the size of a large marble and make very good preserves. They must never be cooked with water as this will spoil them and all the work of gathering such a small fruit would be wasted. They have sufficient juice of their own to cook.

WILD CARROTS

They have no carrot; only the tops can be eaten with other greens.

WILD ASPARAGUS

When small and new, these are very good and taste like tame asparagus. Watch for large fern-like plants that give the appearance of being over balanced by such a large top and small stem. This is asparagus. The new shoots will look like tiny spears peeking up from the ground.

PEPPER GRASS

Pepper grass is good for seasoning when there is no pepper. It is a low leafy plant which is covered with triangular-shaped seeds. The leaves of the plant are more suitable for cooking than the seed.

WILD PIE PLANT

Wild pie plant is a western edible. It has tall, drooping, dull crimson flowers and the leaves are nearly a foot long and narrow into thick stalks. When young, the stalks can be peeled and used like rhubarb and made into a tart pie filling.

MESQUITE

This well-known tree in the southwest has numerous pods much like green beans. When ripe they turn a bright lemon-yel-

FLOWERS
ROSE-PURPLE

WILD ONION

BITTER ROOT

PINE NUTS

low and have a sweet juicy pulp with hard seeds. Desert Indians pound the pod into meal. The raw beans are pleasantly sweet.

SCREW BEANS

A cousin of the mesquite, this bean looks like Mother Nature used a curling iron on it. The screw bean is more sugary than the mesquite. Indians grind the pod into meal and make a very good drink from it.

YUCCA

This plant is rightly called the Candle of the Lord, with its stalk roasted in hot ashes. Flower buds are boiled and make a very fine dish.

EDIBLE ROOTS

ARROWHEAD

You will find this plant growing in shallow water and the leaf is the shape of an arrowhead. Cook it with meat, but do not eat it raw and bitter.

CATTAIL TULE

These are edible boiled, roasted, or eaten raw. They may be dried and pounded into a meal. The Indians of Nevada and California use these a lot.

GREAT BULRUSH

This plant may be eaten raw or cooked or you may dry it and pound it into a sweet flour. The young thick base shoots may be eaten raw.

JACK IN THE PULPIT, OR INDIAN TURNIP

Do not eat this plant raw Baked or boiled it becomes edible. The most satisfactory method is to boil or roast it, dry it and pound it into flour.

CRINKLE ROOT

This is a Dentaria whose roots are crisp and spicy. Eat it raw with salt like radishes.

GROUND NUT

It resembles potatoes in shape, color, odor. Boiled or roasted they become a very wholesome food. Their brownish purple flower has a scent like violets.

JERUSALEM ARTICHOKE
Cooked they resemble artichokes in flavor, thereby getting their name. It is a tuberous plant.

INDIAN CUCUMBER
These may be eaten raw and somewhat resemble a cucumber in flavor.

YELLOW POND LILY OR SPATTERDOCK
You may boil the roots with meat or roast them. The best place to find them in numbers is in muskrat houses, where they store them for winter use. The seeds may be parched and eaten like pop corn.

MAN OF THE EARTH
A cousin of the sweet potato, this has a trailing, climbing vine with flowers like the morning glory. It has tuberous roots sometimes reaching 20 lbs in weight. A large root needs long roasting. The Indians call it Man of the Earth because of its rough resemblance to a man.

PRAIRIE TURNIP
This is a low hairy plant, with long, 5-fingered leaves, has small bluish pea-like flowers. The root looks like a small potato and may be eaten raw in late summer or with salad oil and vinegar dressing. Boiled or roasted they are very fine.

SAND FOOD
A strange parasite growing in southern Arizona, this plant consists mostly of a long fleshy underground stem. During the flowering season it has a small funnel-like top on which are very small purple blossoms. After flowering, it disappears. The underground stem is sweet, tender and juicy. Eaten raw it has the ability to quench the thirst or satisfy the appetite. It may be roasted for a hot meal.

SEA WEED AND KELP
These are good to eat. The kelp is eaten raw while the sea weed that grows on rocks and looks like lettuce is cooked. It is best fried.

ACORNS
The Indians are very fond of these nuts. We gather them in the fall as they drop from the trees. If left on the ground they will get wormy. Keep them in a dry place. To prepare them for eating, crack the outer shells with a rock or other implement and pour hot

water over them, then let them set a while. Repeat twice. The skin
can also be worked from the kernel in a winnowing basket. The fric-
tion against the sides of the basket does it. Sometimes they are roasted
in the shell, then the shell is removed from the meat, and the meat is
ground. In some states the acorns are sweeter to eat and you don't
have to soak them in hot water. I mention the acorn first because it
grows in abundance in so many states. You can grind them into meal
and mix with corn meal or flour or use it in soup along with meat and
beans. Also we make a type of biscuit out of them to eat with meat.

PINE NUTS

The Pinon Pine yields a small kernel nut. That is a favorite with the Washoe and Paiute Indans. It is harvested in California. Nevada, New Mexico and other western states. They knock
the pine cones down on canvas under the trees and take them home in
sacks. Then they lay them out to dry. This harvest takes place in the
fall. After the pine cones are dry they open up and the seeds or nuts
fall out. These are put into shallow pans and roasted. Then they are
ready for market or storage. These pine nuts are sold in stores and are
enjoyed by all people. They can be eaten fresh as a treat, or as the
Washoes do: shell them and make pine nut soup.

HAZEL NUTS

This nut grows on a bush and resembles the filbert in appearance. We always gathered a lot of them in the fall of the year. Some
other well-known wild nuts are hickory, walnuts, beachnuts, and
chestnuts.

WILD FRUITS AND BERRIES

We have several wild berries that we harvested. Of course a lot
of these are eaten fresh but many kinds were dried or in later years
they were canned.

BLUE BERRIES

Picking is still a very important harvest time with my people in Minnesota, and a lot of the harvest is sold. We used to
line the bottom of our buckets with basswood or other large tree leaves
to prevent bruising the berries. Also this helps to keep them fresh. In
the drying of blueberries, we spread them out thin on racks and poles
and boards sometimes using flat rocks. Then the sun did the work. If
the weather was cloudy or damp, then we might have to help the sun.
We placed the flat rocks on a slant and built a fire in the middle of

SAGUARO CACTUS

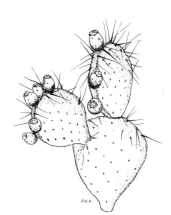

PRICKLY PEAR

them. This helped in the drying process. After the berries were completely dry, we put them in sacks or containers and stored them for the winter.

JUNE BERRIES, RASPBERRIES, STRAWBERRIES, AND BLACKBERRIES

These were all gathered, harvested, and dried in the same way as the blue berries. Now it is more popular to can them.

CHOKE CHERRIES AND PIN CHERRIES

These were dried in the past, but now we make sauces and jellies out of them.

PLUMS

They were eaten raw or pitted and dried. Also we now make jams and sauces out of them and crack the pits and eat the kernels from them.

CRAB APPLES

They are cooked in sauces with a little sweetning to ease the bitter taste. They can also be eaten raw if you like. There are other fruits in some limited areas, but these you can learn best about from the local people. However, I'll mention two unusual ones of the Southwest.

SAQUARO CACTUS AND PRICKLY PEAR CACTUS

These two are good eaten raw, but they are peeled first. Also they can be used for sauces. Some other cactus also have edible fruit. The Saquaro serves as a building material for reinforcing adobe walls and as fuel along with other desert plants. The new shoots of the Prickley Pear can be made into salad, after the stickers are removed. The way to do this is to take hold of the ears with a pincher type clothes pin. Place a bowl of water in front to float the stickers off the knife. Cut the stickers off with the knife, cutting away from you.
There are many wild roots and bulbs that my tribesmen used in different areas. Some as herbs and medicines for different illnesses and others for foods.

BITTER ROOT

A mountain range was named after this plant. This root is very bitter when eaten raw, but is very good when cooked. The Indians harvest it in the spring, and peel off the brown outside bark. They cook it alone as you would potatoes or make a stew with it.

CAMAS BULBS

They are harvested by the Indians. It is a plant found in Oregon, Washington, and Northern California. It usually has blue flowers and grows in mountain meadows and swamps. It grows so thick the whole meadow is changed to blue. They can be cooked as potatoes, but most of my friends roast them. This is done by digging a pit about 2 feet deep. They make a fire in the pit. Use wood that's big enough to make coals. Over this, place green wood with bark on it. Then green leaves or grass and your camas bulbs. Over this put a layer of dirt or sand. If you want really quick results, you can build a fire on this and roast down as well as up. However the heat underneath will do the job. If you only have a few bulbs to roast, wrap them in leaves and put them in wet clay and bake right over the coals. Some Indians would make a pit and line it with rocks. Then they built a fire and heated the rocks very hot, scooped out the fire and placed the green leaves and grass in there. Then they put the camas bulbs in and sometimes they added fish or meat to this fire.

WATER LILY BULBS

They are gathered in Minnesota and roasted.

WILD RICE

It is found in Minnesota, Wisconsin, Michigan, and into Canada, and is often known as Chippewa wild rice, because it is harvested mostly by my tribe. It is called Menomie in the Chippewa language. It's ripe for harvest in September or October.

Rice grows in water so it is necessary to use a boat to harvest it. One person used the pole to steer the boat along through the rice beds. The other person, who we call the knocker or pounder, bends the rice over and with a short paddle, knocks it into the boat. When the boat is full, they take the rice to shore and spread it out on canvas or a floor to dry. The rice has to be turned during this time because it is going through a sweat. It will easily mold and spoil if the air doesn't get to it. We next roast and thresh it. This is done by building a fire under a big iron pot or tub. Then you must keep stirring the rice so it won't burn. Use a paddle stick for this. Leave the rice in until it is dry and roasted. However if you don't have the equipment for roasting, then you can place it where it will dry well and thresh it out after it is dry, and get rid of the beards and hulls to a degree. The threshing is done in what we call the moccasin dance. You stamp the rice with your feet and thresh it. It seems to thresh better while it is still warm from the roasting. But the main thing is for it to be dry. We used to spread it out on lumber or flat rocks and let it dry for days. Wild rice is good in soups, stews, or as a dressing with meat.

WILD OATS

This was used a great deal by the Indians, especially in the western states. This was roasted or singed over a fire to get rid of the long sharp beards. It was then ground into a meal and used for breads or as soup thickening. Many other grass seeds were used in different areas. The Paiute Indians had a large cone shaped basket that they used just for harvesting grass seeds.

MAPLE SUGAR AND SYRUP

The maple sap is taken from the trees in March and April. This is done by cutting a notch into the tree just slightly into the wood. Then a tin trough or spout is attached and by this method the sap is collected into the pail that is hung below. We used half a gallon or gallon cans with a wire attached to the top for a handle. We also used vessels made from birch bark for harvesting this in the old days. The pails are visited once or twice a day, depending on the rate of flow of the sap. After the sap is harvested it is put in a big iron kettle and boiled. The amount of boiling depends on whether you are going to make sugar or syrup out of it. The boiling is done over a slow fire. At the cookoff it is a great treat to take a dipperfull of the thick syrup and drop it into the snow which still is on the ground and make candy for the children.

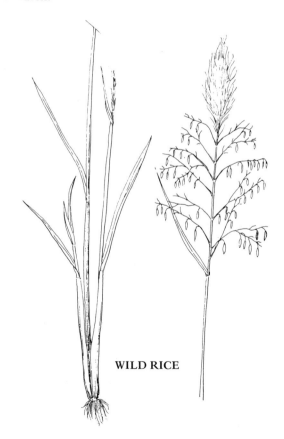

WILD RICE

CHAPTER VI

Knife and a Bag of Salt

Our old timers said "Just give me a knife and a bag of salt, and I can survive in game country." Wearing nothing but breech cloth and moccasins, I have only a hunting knife the first day out. I get some willow bark or I kill a rock chuck with a rock. I have run him down out in a meadow. I cut his hide in strips and, using it as green rawhide, I fasten my knife to a pole. Now I have a spear. When I see ground squirrels or rock chuck sticking their heads out of a hole I stalk them laying flat on my belly at a poles length and spear them as they stick ther heads up again out of the hole. But today I found another weapon; a piece of sharp black obsidian. So I make a spear with it, tying it on with more of my rock chuck rawhide. Now I return my knife to being a knife instead of a spear. For I was afraid to throw it for fear of damaging the point. Now I have a rock hunting spear and can find extra points. If I should lose this one, I can continue to kill chucks and ground squirrels with the knife. But now I can also throw it at rabbits and deer. And I know I can get porcupine along the foothills in the pines. I am saving small points of obsidian to make arrow heads. If I find and kill a deer I shall use his sinews for a bow string.

HOW TO COOK WILD GAME

One thing to remember in cooking wild game is that warm meat has a very strong wild taste that people might not like. In most cases, soaking it in salt water will do the trick. Some kinds have to be marinated and some parboiled in various preparations. All pelts should be saved for future use. Clothing and coverings of various forms can be prepared from them so be careful not to pull the pelt full of holes or cut it in two in the middle, as some people recommend for easy skinning.

MUSKRAT

It may be broiled or made into a delicious stew with vegetables and salt pork added. When meat is half cooked, remove it from the heat and finish it by roasting. Muskrat can be roasted like duck with dressing.

There are musk glands situated inside the forearms and hind legs which should be removed with care, but I have eaten muskrat without doing this, and it still tasted good.

MUSKRAT

RACCOON

OPOSSUM

COON

Scent kernels are situated under the front legs and on either side of the spine in the small of the back. These must be handled with the same care as in the muskrat. Wash the meat in cold water and, depending upon the animal's age, cook it the proper amount of time. Stuff it with breadcrumbs and onions and bake. A coon is very greasy and the bread will absorb the grease, so make sure that the stuffing is dry. If you have an apple and a piece of celery on hand, add them to the stuffing for a delicious flavor. We also used to grind up racoon and mix it with deer meat to make a good hamburger.

POSSOM

Hang it up and bleed it overnight, then clean and draw and allow the meat to hang for three days in a cool place. Boil it with hot peppers in several waters, then roast him with sweet potatoes and sprinkle on salt and pepper and lemon juice while baking or roasting.

BEAVER

Skin it open except for the tail. Beaver tail is a real treat. Clean and broil it over the coals of a hot fire. The scaly skin will come off in blistered sheets, showing a white solid meat. When skin is removed, continue to cook the meat over the coals. The beaver itself is good roasted or cooked in stew.

RABBIT

Clean in lots of fresh water and watch for the hairs that will adhere to the flesh of the rabbit. Boil as in a stew, fry or bake.

SQUIRREL

Prepare the same manner as the rabbit, but it is a bony creature and deserves some special attention. It can be boiled and creamed with small new potatoes and carrots for a delicious meal.

SKUNK

Skunk can be eaten IF you can remove the scent carefully. It must be aired for a couple of days, and I would advise cooking it outdoors. Boil it in many waters with onion, garlic and hot peppers. This appears as if you are masquerading the skunk, but it is very delicious if prepared properly. It takes a long time and a lot of patience to prepare this animal. After the boiling process, grease him heavily and bake him a good long time. The skunk fat should be removed, as otherwise the meat will not taste good.

RABBIT

STINKY

WOODCHUCK

DEER MEAT

It can be prepared much the same as beef, but it is good to cook it with onions or garlic to rid it of the strong wild taste. My squaw wraps a deer roast in fat bacon or tacks suet onto it, as otherwise it gets dry. Some people like the taste of the deer meat, and cook it like beef.

BEAR

Bear meat is best roasted. Clean off all the excess fat. Mountain sheep may be roasted, stewed, broiled, or barbecued like the meat of other game.

LYNX

This animal is considered by many to be far superior to that of the muskrat or posom. The hind quarters are usually roasted and the fore legs made into stew. Stewing is usually best, as most of them are tough.

ALLIGATOR

The tail tastes very much like fish. It is white, quite lean, and rather coarse grained. Broiled gator steaks should be basted often with butter or bacon fat while cooking.

SNAKES

Rattlesnake meat is a delectable dish. General Custer claimed to be the first white man to eat rattlers and he liked it. Brown it lightly in frying pans.

LIZZARDS

Chuckwalla in the Southwest is considered a toothsome morsel if you can catch him. He has a habit of scurrying for the crevices n rocks and once there, blows himself up so tightly that he is difficult to pull free. The best method of getting them is to puncture him with a sharpened stick to let the air out of him. He feeds on young leaves and flowers so his flesh is choice.

CROW

You have heard the expression "He had to eat crow". Well, crow tastes like a combination of duck and chicken and can be made into delicious pies. Old birds should be parboiled first.

OWLS

They can be eaten boiled. In fact, Arctic explorers have said they prefer owl to chicken.

PACK RAT

Pack rat is eaten in Mexico and can be found on the open market. Its flavor resembles that of a young rabbit. Mice also can be eaten broiled over open coals.

PRAIRIE DOG

This little animal is very plentiful and is a very delicious feast. It can be boiled, broiled, baked, or roasted. I have eaten most types of gophers and ground squirrels and the prairie dog is especially good.

GROUND SQUIRREL A LA SHOSHONE

The Shoshone people singe the hair off the squirrels over the open fire. They then roast them over the fire or bake them in coals. When they are ready to eat, they peel back the skin and yank off a leg. A little salt is good on the meat. The Shoshone do not bother to remove the entrails before cooking. They call this dish zip.

Also in the domestic line of meat that I have eaten are horse, dog, and cat. Many Indian tribes in the United States ate dog in the old days. And some still do at certain ceremonial times. As one old trapper buddy of mine once said, "I'll eat anything that don't eat me first, if I'm hungry."

One thing to remember with wild meat—it's a good idea to cook older animals by browning them in a frying pan for flavor and then boil them to get the toughness out. The juices are good for stew or a gravy base.

A FORETHOUGHT ON HUNTING AND TRAPPING

I feel that people who move on to the land in today's time should show greater respect than ever for wildlife. If you go in too heavy for hunting or trapping you will soon deplete all the game in your area. It is much better that you try to raise your own meat—rabbits, goats, cows, chickens and turkeys—and take wild game only as a last resort. Also its definitely not a good idea to trap if you aren't going to eat the meat of the game you get. Our four-legged brothers and sisters are an important part of the future of this country and if you let this thought guide you in your hunting and trapping you will be in harmony with the out-of-doors.

CHAPTER VII
Hunting and Stalking

As a preference of weapons, I like a .22 bolt action rifle for providing the weekly meat larder with small game. I prefer this to automatic as you are not as inclined to waste shells. When deer or big game hunting, I like a 30-30 for open country and use a shotgun in brush country with slugs or buck shot. Sometimes in the brush country, when deer hunting, I still carry a slingshot for small game. Instead of old auto inner tubes, I use a surgical rubber for the slingshot. The new type of inner tube does not have the stretch that the old post-war tubes had. Many a ruffled grouse, gray squirrel or rabbit has found his way to my table, thanks to the slingshot. Back during the depression—W.P.A. days, there was hardly an Indian working on the road crew that did not carry a slingshot to get a little camp meat.

I carry a 16 gauge shot gun for hunting pheasant, ducks, and geese, but find my 410-22 over and under gun as effective for wing shooting and still have a .22 rifle along for other purposes.

I have killed woodchucks, grouse, and rabbits with a bow and arrow as well as deer. Stalking is very important. The closer you get, the better. My tribesmen depended on this way for years, and some of them still do their hunting with the old type obsidian or flint arrowheads. A 45 to 55 pound bow has proven the best with me for all around hunting. However, in this field, there is much variation of choice, and many outstanding archers have other preferences.

Of course, the broad headed hunting arrow or obsidian flint arrowheads is the only thing for big game. For small game, use blunt bullet tipped arrows.

NIGHT HUNTING

I have spent many a fall night out by the corn fields with my dog hunting racoon. He would chase the coon until he treed or cornered it so it would stand and fight. On a fall night, nothing is sweeter to the hunter's ear than the baying of a coon hound, following the trail over hill and hollow around the old swamp. I used to carry a .22 rifle and a 3 cell flash light for this type of hunting. The 3 or 5 cell light with a head that will focus into a fine beam is best. Also we used this type of light for Jack lighting or shining deer in the north country. In some of that territory, the night would sound like a 4th of July celebration,

STALKING GAME

DON'T   DO

WATCH YOUR SHADOW

APPROACH GAME WITH THE WIND IN YOUR
FACE. DON'T LET IT SMELL YOU

HEEL FIRST ON GRASS   TOE FIRST ON ROCK

there were so many night hunters. We used a 12 or 16 gauge long tom
shot gun with buck shot for this business. We would go along the edge
of fields and meadows and shine the light back and forth over a small
area, then turn off the light and walk a little further, then try the light
again. This isn't recommended in states where night hunting is unlawful, or for territory where there is domestic live stock grazing. Most
states make this practice unlawful because it takes the sport out of
hunting. We used this method when we needed meat for food, and
felt justified on that basis, because city hunters often come out later
and shoot only for sport, decreasing our meat supply.

Sometimes we picked a side hill and sat there the night overlook-
ing a meadow, flashing the light on ocasionally to see if any deer had
come out of the woods to graze. This type of hunting is also called fire
hunting. We do it using a wire basket fastened to the end of a 6 foot
pole. You can put pine knots in it and start it off with a little kerosene.
I use this method along a lake shore when I'm out in the boat. The

deer is attracted by the light. His eyes shine at night. We hunt only in the fall of the year. We consider it a very bad thing to kill an animal when it has its young and the fawns still need milk.

OTHER WILD GAME

Elk and moose are hunted similar to deer. Mountain goat and sheep require a lot of stalking too. A friend of mine uses a dog to hunt wild pigs. There are turkey, quail, and prairie chicken. Other edibles in wild game are the mourning doves, coots, or mudhens, jack snipe, and various cranes. Others in basic survival foods, porcupine, bear, possum, rattlesnake, certain lizards and ground squirrels, skunks, prairie dogs, crow, owls, fox, cougar, wolf, lynx, wild cat, coyote, armadillo. Black birds that congregate in great flocks in the fall are good eating too. The best way to shoot them is with either a .22 rifle loaded with .22 shorts, or a shotgun with number 7 or 8 shot.

In hunting game, one should know as much about the country as possible. I find it best to hunt rabbits along creek bottoms and brush thickets in western areas. In woodland country, they may be found around swamps, thick brush and berry patches. The best time to hunt jack rabbits is early evening or early morning. In fact, in Nevada, we hunt at night while driving along the desert roads. One may hunt in late September, and all winter long. This is after the tick and worm season is past, as rabbits contract a sickness called tanarabi from ticks.

When you shoot, be sure you can recover your game. Don't shoot just because it's a clear shot to kill something, and not be able to recover it is a waste of ammunition and good meat. I seldom shoot at rabbits on the run with a .22 rifle for this reason. I try to make a clean, sure kill.

Up in northern Minnesota, we hunted the snowshoe rabbits and cotton tails. The best time for this was October and November. At this time, the snowshoe rabbit turns white, but the ground is still bare of snow, so the rabbits can be easily seen. My brother and I would shoot six or eight of them in an afternoon, and dress and clean them. This would be our meat supply for the week.

In hunting gray squirrels, one should watch for their large leafy nests in the tops of the trees. Then proceed cautiously because once the squirrel knows a person is hunting them, they will start circling around the tree trunk to get away from the person, and to keep out of sight. The red squirrel is easily found because of his chatter, but I pass by this little fellow unless I am very hungry, because he has little meat on his bones.

The ruffled grouse are easy to hunt since they usually fly up into a nearby tree and sit there watching you. You can easily kill them with a .22 rifle. I used to shoot their heads off wth a .22. The best place to find them is near oak trees when acorns are falling or around the wild crab apple tree. Also they like the wild cranberries, and like to fly up into spruce trees. I had a dog that was part spitz and setter, and he was very good at treeing them. When the grouse flew up into the tree, he would sit under the tree and bark at them until I came.

Deer hunting in the woodlands is a waiting game. Either find a water hole where they come down or a good deer crossing and wait. Early morning or evening is best for hunting. There are meadows or small fields where you can stalk them by making the rounds of these water holes and crossings. Be sure to approach with the wind carrying your scent away from the potential game. If you spot a deer, try to keep something between you and the deer, like a tree or a rock. If need be, belly crawl through the grass, and only move when the deer is grazing or looking in a different direction. Some of the old timers used to put salt on the ground to try to attract the deer. This would be the coarse salt or even a small block of salt. The deer would eventually come down for this, but it is a slow business. I've spent all morning trying to get close enough for a shot.

FISHING

The hook and line of course, is perhaps the method most used. For that type of fishing, just be sure you bring along plenty of hooks, varous sizes, and some artificial baits. Flys are always good to have along, and it might be a good idea to learn to tie your own. If you are moving to the wilderness for a home, the supply of materials is near at hand. The deer and squirrel's tails and feathers from birds is all you need with a little string to tie them on. I caught an assortment of fifteen rock bass, sunfish, and perch, using nothing but a piece of white cloth torn off my handkerchief. I was hungry for fish and could find no bait, and the sight of the white piece of rag waving up and down in the water was enough to entice them near to investigate. I'd watch them closely, and when they came near to try a nibble. I'd jerk the line and set the hook, and have my fish.

When the fish go up to spawn in the spring of the year, you can sometimes walk along the stream at night with a flash light and spot them in the water. The wire basket with the pine knots is good for this, where there is no danger of fire. In some states it's legal to spear them both day and night.

Gill netting is another way you can take fish. We use the net two different ways. On a small stream we set the net in one place and let the fish come into it. Or we go up stream and wade and splash, make noise and drive the fish into the net. With two men you can wade the stream with the net between. And still another way is to set the net up in the lake in an area where you know there are fish, and leave and check it in the morning. You must be sure to have enough weights to sink the bottom edge and floats to keep the top up. Also put an anchor on it to keep it from moving. Another way yet is to use baited hooks on a set line or trout line, tied on shore, which you can leave and check in the morning for success.

We also use cone-shaped fish traps made out of willows. Another method along lakes or ocean is to build traps of rocks in shallow water and let the tides or waves bring the fish in. In winter we build fish houses. These are small houses about 4 by 4 and 6 feet tall. They don't need to be too tall since you sit down in it most of the time. By sitting there, you can wait for the fish and spear them. We use a spear made from a 4-tine pitchfork. In this method, a decoy is made in the shape of a fish with a lead weight imbedded in its belly. You work it up and down in the water and soon the fish come near enough to strike. You can also fish with hook and line through the ice using bait. We use lead from old car batteries or lead weights from car wheels, which are used to balance the wheels. I must advise, before trying these methods of fishing, check the law in your locality, as in some states, these methods may be illegal. These methods are used only for survival.

TRAPPING

I used to cover 25 miles a day on foot and sometimes during muskrat season, I was looking at my traps during the night. In the cold northern Minnesota winters, when for days it's 10 to 30 degrees below zero, you become used to it and

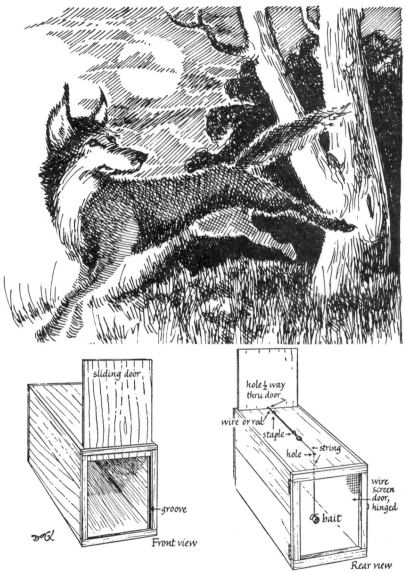

Live box trap. Rod is set at "hair trigger" in hole in door.
Slight jerk on bait string pulls rod, drops door. Important:—
door must slide very freely in its groove, which can be waxed.
Originally printed in *Amateurs Naturalist's Handbook,* by Vin-
son Brown. Reprinted by courtesy of Little, Brown and Company, Boston.

dressed for the weather and a brisk walk across the country
with the sound of snow under foot is a refreshing experience
as you make the rounds from trap to trap. In trapping one
must know as much as possible about the habits of each fur-
bearer along his line, their likes and dislikes, how suspicious
they are of man's smell, what they prefer to eat, do they like
water, brush, or open prairie.

MINK

Mink are found throughout most of the country, and
usually like to live near the water in wooded areas and along
rivers in prairie land. They are good swimmers, but will travel
long distances on land. The mink travels a regular route, so if
you see tracks along your trap line, you can find a good place
that the tracks pass by and make your set there. Their main
food likes are rabbits, squirrels, fish, frogs, mice, chipmunks,
woodchucks, poultry, and muskrats. Their mating season is
February or March and the young are born in April or May.
There are two to ten in a litter.

I start trapping for mink about the 25th of October and
trap through the winter to March 1st as that is when they are
in their prime. I use gloves in setting all my traps and snares
to keep human scent off them. When I set traps in water, I
use lined rubber gloves. Do not disturb the natural appearance
of things any more then necessary. Mink travel along lake-
shores and follow rivers and creeks. They like big swamps with
tall grass where they can find mice and will visit each water
spring in search of frogs. I like water sets for mink. Put your
bait on the end of a forked stick just above water. Pick a place
in a spring or creek where the water doesn't freeze over. Put
2 or 3 traps around the bait. Cover the traps over lightly with
water soaked leaves, grass or moss. Anchor to the stick or
stake and conceal the chain and stake as well as possible. For
dry land I find a hole, log, rock pile, or willow thicket that the
mink have visited. Then I place my bait in such a way that I
can put one or two traps where he will have to step in them in
order to get at the bait. I cover traps over with leaves, grasses,
and dirt that are natural to the area. For bait I use chickens,
rabbits, duck entrails, heads, feet, etc., or fish, squirrel, muskrat, frog, mice, and even the mink itself serves as bait. If I

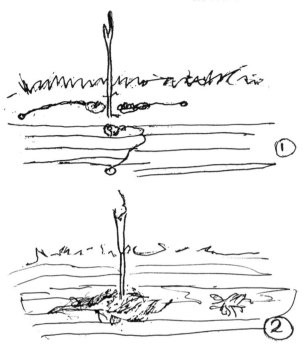

catch one, I find that often I can catch others on his skinned remains. Not that he will eat his relative, but curiosity will cause him to investigate. In killing a trapped mink, crown him or club him so as not to ruin the fur. Wash off dry dirt or blood spots. Skin it with the skin out. Slit down the back of the legs to the vent, then slit down the underside of the tail to the tip. Use a sharp knife for skinning. Work flesh free from the skin with knife and fingers. Be careful not to cut the skin around the front feet and ears and eyes. Around the head is where the real skinning skill is required. Feet and claws should be left on the pelt. I use apple box sides or other thin lumber to make stretchers, but you can buy them from trappers supply houses to get started. You can catch mink in a live or humane trap. Set the trap along a creek. Place the back of the trap with the bait in it against a log or tree so that the mink has to come through the front entrance. Put brush and rocks along the path and slides of the trap so the mink is guided to it.

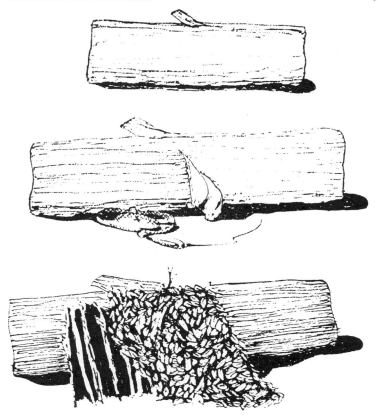

WEASEL

I would advise trapping weasel only in northern areas where he turns white in winter, except for the tip of his tail which remains black. In summer, his color is brown with black tail tip. He's that skinny little animal with black beady eyes. He's a very blood thirsty animal. He is fearless and will fight ferociously if cornered. Like the mink, he is a great traveler and goes many miles in search of food. He likes swamp ground, woodlands, but goes around haystacks, old buildings, brush piles, rock piles, etc. Here he finds mice and rodents and a rabbit now and then. He enjoys traveling after each fresh snow, and you will see his tracks around then. You can distinguish them from squirrels in that he travels along as if he's really going somewhere and doesn't spend all his time in one area. The weasel usually has his den under tree roots or a rock pile. He will also set up housekeeping in the abandoned burrows of another animal as he doesn't dig his own burrow. He will move right in, often killing the former tenant and eating him. He is a menace to poultry raisers, as he not only kills for food, but will kill 8 or 10 hens in a night just for the fun of it. The weasel has 2 or 3 litters a year and from 4 to 8 young at a time.

I start trapping weasel in November and trap through to February. I make my sets around haystacks, hedges, in abandoned burrows, near swamps. The weasel is more hungry than cautious. I put my live trap in the only entrance to the weasel's den, then cover it with leaves, grass and brush. It then serves as either a mink or weasel set. In good weasel country I use regular wood rat traps with an over spring. These are reasonably priced and they kill instantly. I drag bloody meat toward the trap to give the weasel a trail to follow.

Skin him with the skin side out. Cut along the bottom of the back feet, down the legs to the vent and around it. Don't cut down the tail, but merely pull the tail bone out. Leave the feet and claws on the pelt. I make stretchers out of apple boxes. Be sure to make stretchers the right size. Don't over-stretch it or the pelt gets too thin.

SKUNK

Our smelly friend. In the fall of the year when you smell skunk, you know he's been caught in a trap or hit on the highway or had an encounter with a fox or dog. This is where smell tells. The skunk is a profitable asset to the fur trappers. He's the fellow that's black with two white stripes down his back, about the size of a cat. However, to the fur business, there are the pure black, broad and narrow stripes, and the spotted skunk. Skunks live in all sections of the United States. The skunk is proud and unafraid, since his strong scent discourages most adversaries.

They live in dens, burrows in the ground, around rock piles, in hollow logs, under old buildings. Often 6 to 10 live together in one den. They are night hunters for the most part, and can be seen in the early evening going out to hunt. They like grubs, worms, crickets, grasshoppers, mice, rodents, eggs, poultry, and honey bees. Sometimes they hybernate during the coldest months in northern states. They mate in February or March. The litter of young is from four to ten. If the price for skunk is not good one year, I leave them alone because, like all wild life, they do much good in keeping the balance of nature. I mention this because I have seen hunters who shoot skunk just because they are alive and moving or because they smell. Well, I've known people that were a lot more rotten in their ways and I'd rather associate with the skunk, smell and all, even when trapping and this applies to hunting as well. I always leave enough of the specie so that it can reproduce. That way there is always something to enjoy for tomorrow. Nature is my bank and storehouse. If I go around shooting rabbits or other wild life wantonly, then later there will be nothing and I will be hungry. I may repeat myself sometimes, but this is because I feel very strongly about this and want to impress it on the reader's mind.

Skunk can be caught in box traps. You can use boards and line with wire. This keeps them from chewing out. To set trap for skunk is quite easy because he is not very cautious. I make my pen or shelter in the woods country. Sometimes I nail a piece of rabbit or squirrel to a tree and set my trap below it in such a way that he has to step into the trap to get at the bait. I also set them in abandoned animal burrows. To attract the skunk to the set, I drag a dead rabbit or something over the ground along the area I feel the skunk travels. Or if I know where his burrow is, I drag the bait by it. Do not set traps in his burrow, as you might catch one skunk, but the smell and action will scare the rest out, forcing them to leave the area. While if you make sets in different places around the burrow area, but a distance from it, you might catch several. I also make sets around any big animal that has died, such as horses, cattle, sheep or deer, as this always attracts all the wild meat eaters of the area. I always shoot or club skunks. In shooting, use a .22 short cartridge. Before skinning, I wash off any dirt or blood spots and comb burrs or nettles from the fur. Skin him, cased skin-side out. Cut down the back of the legs to the vent. Be careful, around the vent, as this is where scent glands are that give off that strong scent. Cut down underside of the tail to the tip and skin out the tail

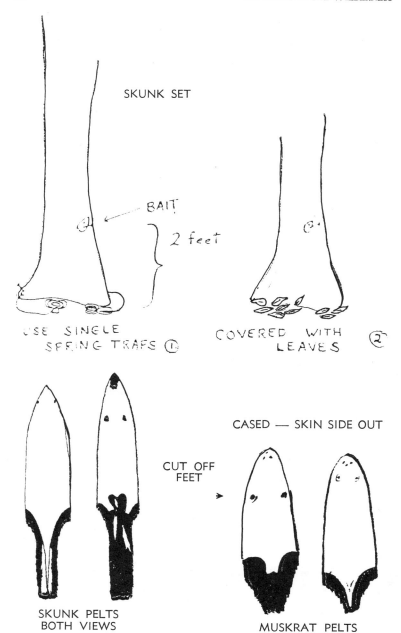

SKUNK SET

BAIT

2 feet

USE SINGLE
SPRING TRAPS ①

COVERED WITH
LEAVES ②

SKUNK PELTS
BOTH VIEWS

CUT OFF
FEET

CASED — SKIN SIDE OUT

MUSKRAT PELTS

from the bone. Pull the pelt off over the head. Be careful and cut right so the skin comes off around ears, eyes, and nose without cutting the hide. Place the pelt on a stretcher and work off the excess fat and flesh with a table knife or other dull knife. The sooner you skin the animal after it's killed, the better, because if you wait, it becomes hide-bound and is hard skinning. We always took the fat from the carcass and saved it and used it either for making soap, or mixed it with other things. It also served as skunk grease and camphor—a home cold remedy.

I make my skunk stretchers of ½ to 1 inch thick boards. Let your pelts dry in a cool, dark place. Keep them away from artificial heat. The skunk fur gets prime from October 20th until March 1st in northern areas. Prime means that it is the winter coat for the animal and the hair will set in the hide and not drop out.

MUSKRAT

The muskrat is one of my greatest sources of income. They are found and trapped in most states. In a fur coat, their dark brown color is often mistaken for mink. The muskrat is an expert swimmer and spends most of his time in or near the water. He is a chunky animal, about 20 to 24 inches long, brown or dark brown with a long, hairless rat tail. He weighs from one to four pounds, I should judge. They are found along marsh swamps, around the shores of lakes and ponds, along streams and rivers. You'll find them anywhere there is water. Right outside of New York City between there and Newark, New Jersey, on the swamp land you see their mud and grass houses right in sight of a million commuters. North of San Francisco in the American River marshes you will also find them. In the New Orleans and Florida Everglades you will find them trapped. They eat cattails, roots, grasses, and will respond to vegetables such as carrots or corn for bait. Muskrats are very prolific; they mate in February or March and their litter of young is 8 or more. They live in dome-shaped grass, mud, and stick houses, built in shallow water. Den entrances are usually under the water. They also live in burrows dug into the banks of rivers and lakes. Those along rivers, the trappers call river rats. Their fur is prime from November 15th on till March 1st, for the best price value. They are mostly night feeders and if you are on a lake in the evening, you'll see them start to come out toward dusk. Their houses and trails through the weeds and muck will let you know where to set traps. Muskrats can be trapped in no stop loss traps if they are placed in the water in their runways and as long as wire or chain is used, so that they can pull out into deep water. The stop loss spring will release knocking them unconscious so that they drown. You can also use the box or cage type live traps baited with carrots, corn or apples. Set it near their runway up on the land and you will have good success.

In winter I set the trap on his sitting shelf in the mudgrass house or little push up. I use a 3 foot stick with a wire attached to it so he can pull it down and drown. He can't pull the pole into the house, so there he is. To dispatch live rats in a trap, I carry a billy club. I look at my rat traps twice a day, once in daylight and again at night.

To skin the muskrat, clean all blood and dirt from the animal and dry him. If the muskrat is frozen, thaw it out before skinning, otherwise you might ruin the hide. Skin him, cased skin side out. Use a sharp knife with a small blade. Cut around the hind feet where the foot joins the leg. Cut down the back of the hind legs to the vent. Cut off the tail and pull the pelt off over the head, working it loose with your fingers. Use a knife around the ears, nose, and eyes. Be careful not to cut the pelt with a dull knife. If you need meat, remember the muskrat is a clean animal with a good diet of grass and vegetables. It tastes like wild duck and it is sold as marsh rabbit in some cafes, at a very high price.

RACCOON

This is the fellow whose face looks like he's wearing a burglar mask. Raccoon are found in most states, but are often thought of as belonging in the southern states. However, in the northern areas in recent years, they have become regarded as a good income for the trapper. Night hunting of raccoon is enjoyed by many hunters. I trap them both for their fur and meat. They are good climbers and swimmers and like to live around swamps, lakes, and streams. They are mostly night hunters and will hibernate during cold weather. They make their dens in willow thickets, hollow trees, and rock

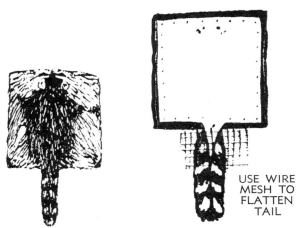

USE WIRE
MESH TO
FLATTEN
TAIL

RACOON PELTS

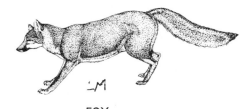

FOX

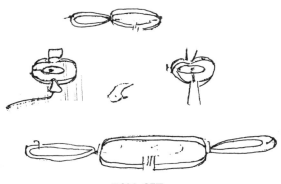

FOX SET

caves. They eat berries, nuts, fruits, bugs, fish, frogs, snakes, and corn. In the fall, corn is their favorite. When you see the corn stalks knocked down along the edge of the field and the corn eaten off the ears, more than likely there are raccoon around. Raccoons have from 4 to 6 young which are born in April or May. I start trapping and hunting raccoon in late October and continue through January. I use two traps to a set. I dig down two or three inches in the ground. This way, when I set the trap, I can cover the spring and chain over with dirt. The jaws and pan are then sprinkled over with dirt and covered with corn silk and grass. I have taken plenty of raccoon with this set. Also have caught fox and skunk where I've set for raccoon. I always use gloves because some of those old coons are cagy, and will not come near a trap that has the human scent.

Along creeks I throw brush around so that a raccoon that is following the water in search of fish and frogs, has to go into my trap. With the brush, I block off all spaces except one trail, and there I place the traps. Sometimes I arrange this in such a way that I can use a tree or log and make a pen set out of it, then I use fish or frog for bait or other meat and sprinkle fish oil in the area. Another set I use is where a log has fallen across a stream and there are signs that animals are using it to cross, I set my trap where the animal would be most apt to step. If the log is rotten on the end, I dig out the decayed wood and place the trap right on the end of the log. Then I cover the trap over lightly with moss, leaves, or grass. Sometimes I drag bait across the creek or the log. In baits I've used rabbit, fish, poultry entrails, feathers and feet. Also corn, tomatoes, melons, eggs, clams, apples, and nuts. The raccoon also likes berry patches and orchards. He has a sweet tooth so if you have bees, you can use honeycomb.

I always wash and clean off any dirt or blood from the fur, then dry it well with an old towel. The raccoon is skinned open-cut around the hind foot at the ankle. Cut down the back of the leg to the vent. Cut down the under side of the tail to the tip, and down the belly to the under lip. Cut down the front legs and cut the front feet off where the leg joins the foot. There will be a lot of flesh and fat on the pelt. Remove it, using a dull knife. I have several pieces of plywood

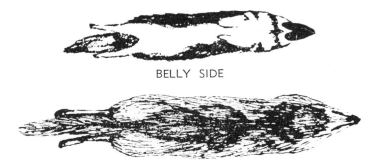

BELLY SIDE

FOX PELT

that I use to stretch my raccoon on. I use carpet tacks to tack them down. In stretching, I try to get a square effect. Hang it in a dry cool place and check it from time to time while it is drying. Wipe off excess oil that forms. Raccoon can be caught with humane traps. Build your own box trap and line it with wire. Make a trap door that will swing in and then release. You must have a long one, about 3 feet long, to catch raccoons. However, hunting with a good coon hound at night is more fun and rewarding. That activity is something the coon hound can teach you better than I can.

Fox, coyote, wolves and beaver are in dwindling supply, and are important to the ecological balance so while we will continue to include information in regard to their habits, we have deleted all reference to trapping. However, in case you should shoot one out of need for the meat and skin, we have included the information on skinning.

FOX

Here, to me, is one of the hardest animals to catch. His cunning and slyness have made him the character of song and legend. The expressions "sly like a fox" and "Kinda foxy" are tributes to his talents.

The fox is found throughout North America. There are a number of varieties: red, white, silver, black, cross, gray, and swift. The red fox is the one I've had most of my experience with, but what applies with him is true of the others for the most part. The fox is principally a night hunter, but likes early morning, late afternoon, and evening times as well. They like mice, fish, rabbits, birds, squirrels, rodents, grasshoppers, poultry, and fruit at times. The fox raises from 3 to 10 pups which are born in April or May. Their dens are usually in the burrows of other animals they have taken over and enlarged. They seem to prefer a hill or hillside, but will sometimes have their den around swamps under the roots of trees. They are great travelers and cover long distances during their nightly food hunt. Except when they have young, they don't use their den too much. They will make their bed along their trail in tall grass at one time, under a brush pile another time, or lay down on the wooded hillside. The fox is very smart, but he is also curious. If you follow his trail for a ways, you will see where he turns out to investigate a bush here and a clump of dead grass in another place. I look along old cattle trails, bare spots in fields and hilltops, along old abandoned roads, and dry creeks, and swamp bottoms for fox tracks.

In skinning fox, they are skinned flesh side out. Leave the feet and claws on the pelt. Cut down the foot and the back of the back left to the vent. Cut down the tail to the tip and skin it away from the tail bone. Pull the skin off over the head. Put it on stretchers and scrape off excess flesh and fat with a dull knife. Sometimes I use a sharp knife to skin off the hide flesh from the pelt. Put it on the stretcher, skin side out. Be sure and tack down the tail flat so air gets to it. After it's almost dry, turn it, fur side out, and let it finish drying. Keep fox pelts in a dry cool airy place.

WOLF OR COYOTE

The great wolf or timber wolf is found mostly in the western and woodland states. I know there are still some in northern Minnesota and Michigan. Of course, they range into Canada and Alaska. The coyote or prairie wolf is found in all our western states.

The wolf is a traveler and will cover great distances during the course of a hunt. And since he has no permanent den or home except while raising his family, he has more maneuverability in his search for game. When he gets tired, he just curls up and sleeps on the ground. The skinning and stretching process is the same as for the fox.

BEAVER

This is the big cousin of the muskrat. A big brown fellow with a broad, flat tail that he uses to slap the water in warning or as support when he stands up and chews down big trees. He has large web-feet for swimming. He is a great dam builder. You can determine if he's in an area, if there are mud and stick dams across the streams or large mud and stick dome-shaped houses. His main diet is grass and tender bark of trees. In skinning, the tail and feet are cut off and the skin is opened down the belly. For scraping hides, get a round headed post about eight inches thick and tie the hide as shown in the diagram and scrape it with a dull knife. Keep the hide wet while scraping it and scrape off the hair and gray outer skin until it shows white.

BEAVER PELT

All small animals are skinned cased and larger ones are skinned open, sliced down the back legs and down the belly. In dressing out meat, cut the pelvis bone and down belly to chest and remove entrails. Cut off head, feet, and tail. Cut to frying size or for storage.

The animals listed before are your principal fur bearers. However, bear and cougar can be trapped also. They are cautious, but require special traps of a larger size. Wild cat and lynx can be taken in the same method of traps as fox. In looking for good markets for furs, send for a sample copy of Fur, Fish & Game, 25C, 2878 E. Main St., Columbus, Ohio 43209. Many fur buyers advertise in this magazine.

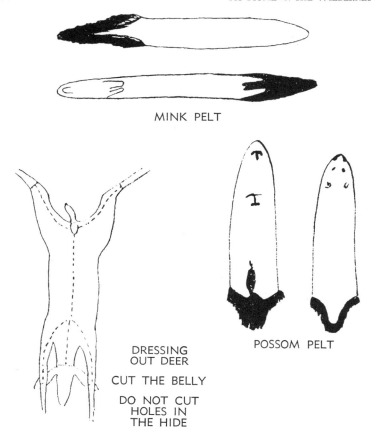

MINK PELT

DRESSING
OUT DEER

CUT THE BELLY

DO NOT CUT
HOLES IN
THE HIDE

POSSOM PELT

My mother used racoon fat for baking and cooking. Also she mixed deer meat which is rather dry with racoon which is fat—a very good hamburger resulted.

TANNING AND PRESERVING

After the hide is taken from the deer, one must flesh it, (remove the fat and flesh), then stake it out and stretch it to dry. The tanning process may be started immediately.

There are different ways to tan. One is to soak the hide in a water and wood ash solution for about two weeks or until the hair begins to slip. One friend of mine uses just plain water for soaking the hide. Then pull it out and scrape all hair off and rinse it in clear water to remove dirt, hair, etc. After the hide is clean, use a mixture of brains (the brains are cooked and the juice off them is worked into the hide. Work into hide back and forth and use this treatment until it is soft and pliable. After you have worked the brains into the hide, rinse off the surplus in clean water. Then, using a smooth post with the bark off, slip or see-saw the buckskin back and forth until it is soft and dry.

Then you build a cone or teepee shaped support out of poles and tie the skin over it. Build a small fire, smoking it the way you want, reversing sides according to the desired color. This also helps to cure it.

Another method is to use a strong soap solution in the water for soaking, and the rest of the tanning process is the same.

FOODS

In the north country you will find that a smoke house or outside shed often serves for keeping meats and other good products frozen for long periods of time. In smoking meats or fish, always use hard woods, never use pines or resinous wood, as the meat will taste like it.

FUEL

In the prairie and desert areas, dry cow dung which we call cow chips can be used successfully for fuel. Many old timers up in the Dakotas and Montana used this.

CHAPTER VIII

Trail Wise Trail Ways

When you are going to go farther than eyesight from your camp in the wilderness, you must remember to blaze a trail in one of the most accepted ways. Do not rely on your sense of direction or land marks alone, as when in the wilderness, there is more than one stone, tree or stump that looks alike and your directions soon become garbled.

When blazing and using live trees, be careful not to chop or disfigure the tree permanently. A bark cut such as shown in the diagrams will be sufficient. Broken twigs or branches can be used in much the same manner indicating directions in which your trail was traveled. When returning to camp, if the sign says you made a left turn going, then you must make a right turn coming back. Do not become confused and perhaps turn the wrong direction.

Grass tied into knots indicating direction is very satisfactory, as this is perhaps the only method that will not be disturbed by traveling animals, with the exception of the tree blaze. Rocks could be easily knocked down or twigs trampled on and moved so that the direction is lost.

If you do become lost, do not travel after dark. You are sure to become confused. Think to yourself that you are not lost, your encampment is lost. Make yourself as comfortable as possible. Build a fire, and perhaps you could find some wild grasses or roots that are edible to chew and curb your hunger pangs if you didn't take any food with you. Cut some boughs from trees or gather fallen leaves and make yourself a bed. Cover yourself with dry leaves and sleep.

If on the following day you cannot find your marked trail, then climb up to a high hill or tall tree and try to locate some landmark you remember. Perhaps there will be camp smoke indicating there are other humans about. Take your bearings and start out. If you use the sun for a compass, you cannot become lost. In winter months the sun travels slightly to the south but it still rises in the east and sets in the west. In late summer, the sun travels slightly to the north. Keep the sun in line with your face. As the afternoon wears on, keep the sun directly to your back. In this manner you will come to your chosen destination. There are plants and herbs that will tell you in which direction you are traveling. Moss grows on the north side of a tree. The tops of fur or spruce trees point to the east. Golden Rod points to the north. Prickly lettuce has leaves that point north and south.

The stars are perhaps the greatest and most adequate compass at night. The seamen and Indians have used them for centuries as positive guides. The most easily recognized in the star groups is the Big Dipper, located in the northern region. The Dipper revolves around a smaller group of stars known as the Little Bear. The two stars forming the edge of the cup are called pointers, pointing to the North Star. This star is located in the tail of the Little Bear.

A pileated Woodpecker digs its holes in the east side of a tree. The flying squirrels choose the east side hollows of trees for their nests. The north side of a hill is often moist and mossy so there is less noise in walking than when on the south side of the hill. This is an old Indian trick. He travels incessantly at night and never seems to become lost. He never needs a compass, as nature has provided him with one in various disguises. Spiders choose the driest and warmest side to erect their webs, which naturally is on the south side.

Ducks, geese, and other water foul seem to prefer the west side of lakes and streams for breeding. Frogs, minnows and fish favor the west side, too.

If you can find a source of water such as a spring or water hole, camp close to it, and the birds and animals will give you a source of food and in time, you can learn from them what is good to eat of the plants there too.

If, by any of these methods, you cannot find a lost camp, then do not continue to wander about confused. Do not panic, as this is very bad. Simply sit down and relax, taken inventory of your pockets for any useful items, and make yourself comfortable. Build two fires, 50 feet apart and try to remain as much as posible between the two fires, as this is where searchers will look. To occupy your time, tend the fires alternately, going first to one and then the other.

Try to capture a ground squirrel or other edible animal. Or if fish are near-by, try noodling for them if you haven't anything to catch them with. Noodling is a simple procedure and a great sport. Tie something white and small onto your hand securely and place both hands quietly beneath a fallen log in the water or near a group of rocks. Wait. Soon you will actually see the fish approaching the waving white flag. They will get closer and finally close enough that you can catch them with your bare hands.

If you are plant wise, gather sufficient foods to last you a day or two. Build yourself a lean-to shelter and try to improve on your camp grounds with every move. Be sure to dig yourself a latrine so that you will not be bothered with insects. To me, the simple way to handle it is to dig what we call a cat hole for when you must relieve yourself and then cover it over. This way you show respect for others that use the area.

As a general rule, you will be found within 48 hours, as there are several good rescue teams that do fast work. But don't take chances. Besides preparing for a long stay, you have been so busy that you have forgotten the passage of time.

Remember when you go hiking in the wilderness, take a good hunting knife, matches, sufficient food for two meals, and warm clothes, just in case your "camp gets lost."

SHELTERS AND CAMP SITES

There are certain basic things to consider in a camp site, depending of course upon your length of stay. Water and fuel are both important. You can, of course, transport both some distance, but this is inconvenient. In locating a camp site, I like to find either a good spring or stream near. The spring is preferred, for in flash floods or run offs there is less chance of the water being contaminated. The main fuel of most woodsmen is wood, so locating near a supply of timber for fire wood is important, and it is also important for building a shelter.

For temporary shelters, take advantage of local natural aids such as large boulders, cliffs or hill sides, caves, and in the woods, wind falls of trees. These aid in basic survival against the elements. Many a man has been saved from a blizzard or sand storm by knowing about some shelter. When you are carrying only a small canvas shelter, it can help provide shelter for you and your provisions. Remember in rainy country to hide away some fire wood where it will stay dry. It sure is good to have dry wood to start a fire on a rainy day.

BUILDING CAMP FIRES

Find a spot completely bare of vegetation. Then, using rock, you build a small circle to contain your fire. Always be sure you have removed all inflammable materials from the area. There are several ways to build a succesful camp fire. See the diagrams on this. One is the pyramid or tepee type. Start building the fire with either paper, grass, bark, tinder, pine cones, or shredded small twigs or wood. Pile larger sticks on top as shown. Another way is to lay two large sticks or logs

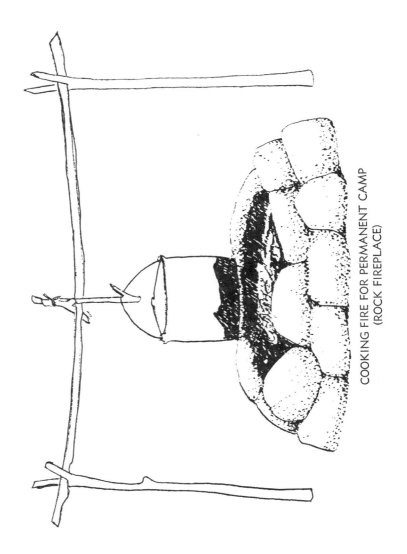

COOKING FIRE FOR PERMANENT CAMP
(ROCK FIREPLACE)

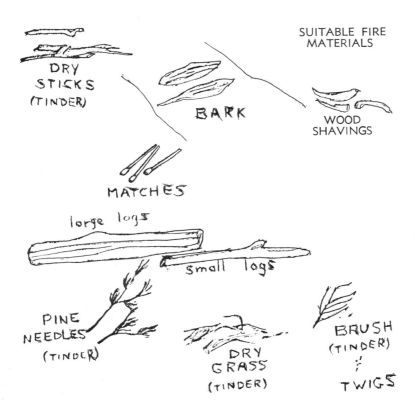

DRY
STICKS
(TINDER)

SUITABLE FIRE
MATERIALS

BARK

WOOD
SHAVINGS

MATCHES

large logs

small logs

PINE
NEEDLES
(TINDER)

DRY
GRASS
(TINDER)

BRUSH
(TINDER)

TWIGS

about 1¼ feet apart. Then place others on them crossways, placing your tinder between the two large sticks. Here are some various ways to hang pots or rest pans for cooking. The tepee or tripod is good for holding pots. Another way is to put poles with a crotch in the ground on the back side of the fire and run a pole between them. Then you can extend a second pole over the fire with another forked post for support and anchor the end with a stake and lashing, or under a log or rock.

LOG WINDBREAK REFLECTS HEAT.

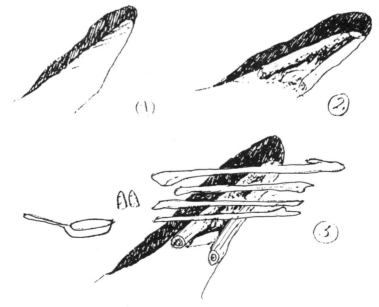

STEPS FOR BUILDING A PIT FIRE.

TEPEE FIRE AND
COOKING TRIPOD

BUILDING A TEPEE FIRE.

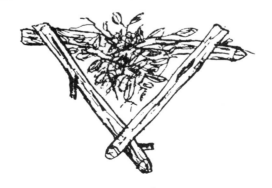

1

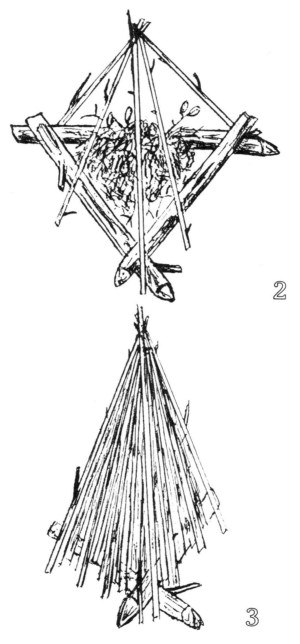

BUILDING A FIRE IN THE SNOW

When building a fire in the snow, clear the snow away from your chosen spot down to the bare ground, then build your fire. Where this is not possible, such as on ice or very deep snow, build a platform of larger logs, or, more preferably, green wood. This will not burn so easily under the fire and will keep your fire from sinking down in the snow. Always try to tramp the snow down and hard-pack it in your camping area. Also put poles or brush under your camp equipment. This will keep it from freezing down. In snow country, if you can find any dry grass, leaves, spruce, evergreen boughs, put these in your bed. They will help to keep you dry and warm.

TEMPORARY TENTS AND LEAN-TO

In tents, one has a large selection from one man pup tents and lean-tos to large tents suitable for family living where even cooking can be done inside. You can also have a canvas floor. In rainy areas, always be sure to dig a trench around the tent for drainage. When making camp in any place, never camp on a dry creek or wash. A flash flood can come in the night, and it has happened sometimes, even in the desert, washing away the camp completely.

When setting up camp on a lake or in woodland areas, pick either a knoll or point where you can get some breeze that will drive away bugs and insects in the evening. Otherwise you will have to build a smudge over your fire. This is done by putting green grass on it to make it smoke.

Lean-to camps should be built with a clear view to the east and the early morning sun.

PERMANENT SHELTER — LOGS OR RAILROAD TIES

CHAPTER IX

Permanent Shelters

Permanent shelters include log cabins, slabwood, adobe, sod, dug-out, birchbark, railroad ties, brush, grass and mud, Eskimo snow igloo, board frame upright.

In building permanent shelters in the wilderness or brush country area, one uses the materials close at hand. In cases of basic survival or lack of money to buy things from a store, you have to know how to build without manufactured products. The early settlers notched logs and bored holes in them using a hot iron or hand auger. They carved and sharpened hardwood pegs with an axe. In this way, they fastened their axe-hewed logs together. Some of these cabins still stand today.

LOG CABIN

By picking logs of uniform size, there was less hewing needed to match them. Chop off the knots, trim down the limbs and ends slightly. The chinking between logs can be either moss, mud, clay, and even cow dung is used successfully. Taken while it's fresh, especially in the winter, it serves to block out cold wind from coming in between the logs.

The roof is made with poles laid criss-cross for better support and then thatched with birchbark. Main support poles can be lashed down with willow bark. Also poles or rock must be placed over the bark to keep it in place. Where bark is lacking, brush and dirt will serve the purpose. In places where you are near lumber mills or where a logging industry has been, you can get slabwood as inexpensive material for construction. This is considered waste material at the mills, or it is the wood that has been cut off by the saw and still has the bark on it. It can be used either with the bark on or off. However, if the bark is peeled off, the wood will hold up better and not rot so easily, especially in wet climate.

The slabs can be used either length ways or vertically. If you use it vertically, the slabs are nailed to the frame. Then the cracks between are covered by other slabs. Used horizontally, you can cover it over with tarpaper and then use edgings (the thin edge that is cut off the boards at the saw mill when they cut the bark off.) This is also throw-away lumber. The roof can be done of the same, but pick even sized slabs and use a heavy grade of roofing paper. Otherwise, you'll have leaks.

ADOBE CABIN

Adobe construction is better suited to the dry southwest where there is less rain to wash away the adobe. The adobe block is made of adobe clay or mud mixed with grass or straw to hold it together. The adobe blocks are 1 foot by 1 1/4 feet or larger depending on how thick a wall you want to build. To make the blocks, you will need a mold or form the size of the block you want to make. Use wide or tight fitting boards for the bottom. The sides should be a one by four. After each block has been packed full and even with the adobe in the mold, after it is formed in the mold, place it on the ground or on a rock to dry. It takes about 3 days for the blocks to dry. When building, more adobe mud is used as mortar to fasten the blocks together. The roof is a combination of poles and mud with large beam supports as posts or room dividing walls, for extra roof support. The Navajo hogan is another adobe type dwelling, only the mud and poles are interwoven. Small poles or brush thatch are used for the round roof. Then mud is packed over it.

SOD SHANTY

This type of dwelling was used by the early settlers on the plains where lumber was hard to get or they couldn't afford it. The native prairie sod was cut into one and a half to two feet wide strips. Then it was placed on top of each other in layers to form the walls for the sod shanty. It was a very warm shelter against the winds and cold blizzards of the plains. Windows would depend also upon the financial condition or nearness to town of the builder. The windows were often covered over with cow skin and left open during the better weather.

DUGOUT

The dugout was dug into a side hill. This hill dwelling had a door facing either north or east and maybe a window on that side for light. With solid dirt on three sides, it was a very warm dwelling.

RAILROAD TIES

Another cheap supply of construction material in some areas is railroad ties. They can be used the same as logs.

ROCK HOUSES

For the man who has the time, rock construction is good. It's lasting, fire proof, and has beauty. It never needs to be painted. Some people combine rock with railroad ties.

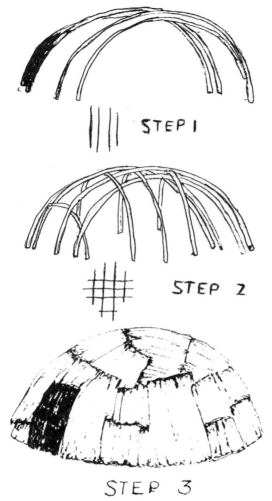

STEP 1

STEP 2

STEP 3

BIRCH BARK

Indians of the Great Lakes and Canada use birchbark to make a permanent dwelling. The wigwam is a round type dwelling. The main framework is made of poles that are anchored in the ground. Then the poles are bent over and lashed together on the top. It is best to use green poles for this type shelter. Other poles run around the framework, horizontally. The bark is then laced to the frame in the old days with deerhide thongs or roots of tamarack.

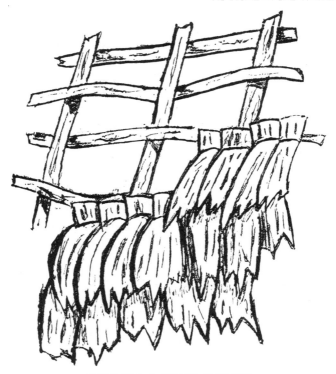

BUILDING A GRASS SHELTER

REEDS AND GRASSES IN SHELTERS

Here you make a frame of poles and then tie long tile or swamp grass together in bunches using these as thatching. The Seminoles thatch their dwellings this way and call it a chickee, while the Pomo and California Indians call it a Wickiup. The Apache make their dwellings of brush which is a wind break and somewhat of a protection in cold weather.

RAMMED EARTH FOR BUILDING AT LOW COST

Rammed earth has proved a great money saver for those who do not have much money. Also it is a fire proof material, good insulator for both heat and cold, and can be made beautiful.

A different but wider variety of soil may be used than for adobe. Any sandy loam with 30% to 70% sand content will do. Many buildings built of rammed earth in this country have stood for centuries

BENT WILLOW AND CANVAS SHELTER

without anything added to the soil. For more durable surfaces it is advisable to use one part of regular cement to 12 parts of dirt. Floors have also been made of it. This cement will stabilize and resist pressure water streams. Oil stabilizers are also available.

The method of construction is simple. Forms made of wood or some material two inches thick are necessary, and spacer boards to hold the forms apart at each end, and wooden clamps that fit on outside of the forms to hold them together. A tamper is needed to pound the damp mixture of soil down in the firm. A wooden block with a broomstick handle or a flat piece of iron with pipe welded to it for a handle will work. The face of the tamper should be about 4 x 6 inches.

A pile of soil that is wet down good will be just right after it stands overnight. To test squeeze a handful, if it holds together it is right. Then drop it, if it splatters it is too wet. If it crumbles it is right. Mix in the cement and tamp the mixture into the wall form. In the spring the soil is usually just right as you dig it out of the earth.

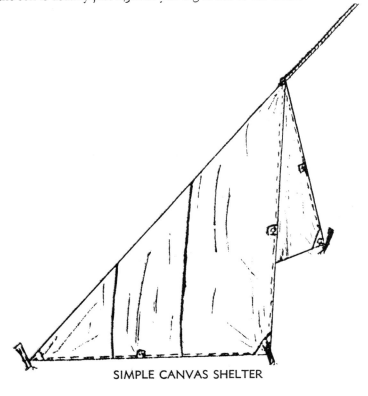

SIMPLE CANVAS SHELTER

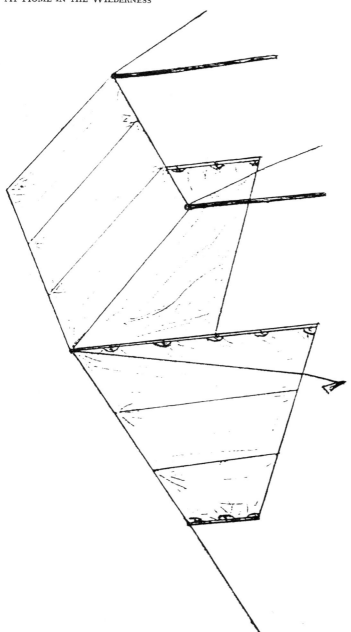

PERMANENT CANVAS SHELTER

ESKIMO SNOW HOUSE

This is made of ice or packed snow blocks cut in sections and laid on top of each other. They are slanted in. This is done by cutting the blocks wider on the end that will face outside. They are sort of wedge shaped. The final block fits in like a cork, wider at the top. To keep the cold air out, they make a tunnel of snow and ice. Sometimes the entrance has a skin flap for real blizzard weather. Using seal oil lamps for heat and light, their clothing keeps them warm, and little heat is needed.

HOME OR CAMP SITE

Finding a camp site or place to live, there is a variety of ways to find a place. Different government agencies have land available. The park service has summer camp sites. In the national forests there are year 'round or summer homes. Also in most national forests, you can pack into wilderness areas and stay as long as you want. The Bureau of Land Management has land available in almost every state. Some you can buy and others you can lease.

In Alaska, many thousands of square miles are there. In many areas there are old abandoned logging or miners' cabins that one can just move into.

In northern Minnesota and some western states, we had cabins offered us to stay in just for looking after the place.

In Canada there is tax land for sale. Also most states have tax land for sale. So if you're tired of trying to survive in the city with rent and riots (or both), take to the brush country. Maybe I'll stop in for a cup of coffee one day.

CHAPTER X

Fire and Firemaking

Whether traveling down a road, camping, or starting out from scratch to build yourself a place in the wilderness, it is important to have a great caution with fire. Fire is the greatest destroyer of wild life, game and plants known to man. Do not throw lighted matches or cigarettes out of a car window or leave a campfire unattended. When building a fire, always remember that a fire will burn several inches into the ground because of the rotted leaves and twigs.

Scrape deep into this top soil and make a clearing large enough to make your fire safe, or build it on top of a flat rock large enough to contain it. Don't think for a moment that a fire will be safe without clearing it, regardless of how little debris there seems to be. Fire will burn underground and break out on some part of the woods other than where the fire was started. This type of forest fire is undetectable until the damage is already done and you are unaware that you are the one responsible for destroying the very property where you were going to build yourself a new home.

There are several ways and methods of starting a fire to cook on. Most people take the simplest method which is a kettle fire. You place tinder in a small area and stack wood on end around it causing a little "stove" to be built around the tinder. Tinder is such items as paper, wood, bark, twigs, fuzz sticks, dead grass, pine needles, leaves, etc. A kettle may be hung or placed over the fire in many different ways to cook. Some people prefer to ring their fire with rocks to make it safe and build the fire in the center.

A trench fire is perhaps about the safest fire. Dig a trench long enough to contain your fire and line the sides with flat stones. Build the fire in the center of the trench. There is more cooking surface than in a common type of fire, such as described above.

A hunters fire is created by placing two heavy logs about two feet apart and building the fire between them. Reflector fires have a log backing so that the heat is reflected in the proper direction.

A star fire is perhaps the oldest method of fire known to man. It has long been used by the Indians and is easy to maintain. When the logs are first started, they are placed in a star shape and as the log burns away, they are shoved toward the center continually feeding the fire.

A tepee fire is more difficult to construct but it is very adequate. Form a triangle with three short logs and place in the center, tinder, a fuzz stick, or dry leaves. Then form a tepee frame over this with light twigs and limbs from fallen trees. Continue to fill in around the original frame until there is just an opening left to light the fire through. It should be a small fire. There is an old saying among the Indians: "White man build big fire, stand way back. Indian build small fire, get real close."

Bonfires or large fires are not necessary unless they are for beacon fires when lost. Never build a fire that can easily get out of hand. All fires that are built have the same basic materials and is started the same way, with fire. They are just constructed differently for better serviceability. Just remember not to leave a fire unattended and always drown your fires with water, stir, and drown them again. Then cover them with fine dirt to make sure they are out. We, as well as you, love the land and its natural beauty, so let's take care of it.

CHAPTER XI

How To Make Soap

Be sure to cover your nose and mouth before mixing lye and other ingredients. Have crockery bowls or small jars for mixing, and a large crockery jar or small wooden tub or pail, and a wooden paddle to stir with.

Disolve 1 can of lye in 1 quart of cold water. (Be sure it is COLD water) in a crockery bowl or small jar.

Have 1/3 cup of ammonia, 1 tablespoon of powdered borax, 2 tablespoons of sugar, ¼ box or 1 cup of Sal soda. If Sal soda is lumpy, be sure to crush out lumps before adding to other ingredients. Then add ¼ cup of boiling water and mix all of these ingredients together.

Heat 5 pounds of lard just enough so it will pour. The lard should be free of salt. Pour the lard into the larger crockery jar or wooden container. Then add the dissolved lye stirring well with the paddle as you add it. Then add the rest of the ingredients and continue to stir until it becomes thick as honey.

Then pour into molds or a lined peach crate, and as soon as it's set it can be cut into bars but leave overnight in its mold, then take it out and put the bars on brown paper far enough apart to allow air between them and them to dry and cure.

This soap will float. It is not as harsh to the hands as some homemade soaps are. Other animal oils, such as raccoon oil, have been used in this recipe. It makes a nice fine-grained soap resembling Fels Naptha soap.

Salt may be removed from lard by placing the lard in a large kettle with water and heating it enough so the lard is melted and set aside to cool. Skim off the lard. Be careful because lard will catch on fire easily.

CHAPTER XII

Equipment for Living In Bush Country or Isolated Territory

FOOD

dried beans
Clifton's multipurpose food
peas
lima beans
salt pork
salt
sugar
cocoa
corn meal
flour
barley for coffee
jello
dry milk
dry eggs
pancake mix
pork and beans
canned milk
sardines
tea

dried or parched corn
unpolished or brown rice
syrup
molasses
margarine
potatoes
spices
vinegar
soda
raisins
prunes
apples, dry
apricots, dry
wheat—150 lbs. per perso
soybeans
matches
soap, laundry and toilet
or lye for when you mak

TOOLS

ax
files, broad and 3-cornered
hunting knife or butcher knife
good pocket skinning knife
assorted nails and hammer
water pails
wash tub
wash board
kerosene lantern
heavy snare wire
saws, carpenter and hacksaw

garden seeds
hoe
spade
traps
mesh wire for making tra
2 doz. stop loss Victor tr
1 doz. overspring rat trap
5 gal. kerosene can or lar
snare wire, lightly woven
hand grinding mill for wh
pliers

MEDICINES

Band Aids
bandages
tape
aspirin
Vicks
Unguentine
Denver mud (or other multi
   purpose poultice)
snake bite kit
iodine
liniment

turpentine for use on insect
   bites, and to clean pine pitch
   from your saw.
alcohol
scissors
needles
tweezers
sewing kit
insect repellent
eye drops

Cooking equipment
cooking pots—enamel or stainless steel—5 sizes
baking pans
cookie sheets, 3
3 bread or biscuit pans
dutch oven for roasting meat or big deep bread pan
cast iron skillets, enamel coated or stainless steel
meat fork, big spoon, soup ladle
storage or serving bowls with leak proof lids
table ware—forks, knives, soup spoons, teaspoons
plates, cups—many prefer tin or granite ware
   linen and bedding—dish towels and sheets have been made out
   of flour sacks by my friend; also they make good dish towels.

Take along hooks and locks for doors as you may either build or use
   an old mine or abandoned logger's cabin, many of which you can
   get the use of for free or very little money

Guns and shells, if you intend to use a shot gun or deer rifle a lot.
   It may be that you would want to look into the possibility of re-
   loading your own.

Bow and arrow men would certainly take extra bow strings and arrows, also extra arrow heads. And check into local woods and
   what the Indians used locally.

Also good supply of rope for packing and loading pack animals, if
   you intend to use them.

Rock salt for salting meat.

Water proof containers for matches, both for storage and camping. The tin ones are best.

Also air and water proof containers for flour, sugar, corn meal, oat meal, beans.

And if you are taking a sling shot be sure to carry extra bands.

Scissors, fishing line, hooks, leaders.

Gun oil, cleaning rod for cleaning guns.

TRANSPORTATION

A jeep or pick-up truck is preferred by the author, but a good serviceable car or panel truck will do. However, most modern cars won't take the back-woods roads and it might cost you a lot in oil pans in the long run. It's a good idea to carry extra gas along and maybe even keep 5 or 10 gallons on hand if you are going into an area where there might be a lack of fuel or until you get a wood stove set up. It's good to take a Coleman camp stove along and some prefer the Coleman lantern for light.

Clothing will be a matter of choice and judgment, and will depend on the climate.

Note for taking along flour, sugar and salt, I've found small canvas bags are good as they don't take as much room as cans. The heavy Bemis grain bags are good for storing flour in, and for beans and corn in large amounts. Of course you will have to watch for mice in case they chew through the bags. I always take a few mouse traps up for that reason.